P9-CQK-343

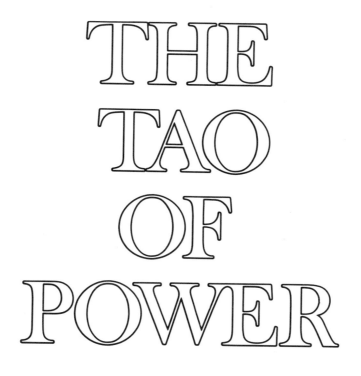

THE
TAO
OF
POWER

THE
TAO
OF
POWER

A Translation of the *Tao Te Ching* by Lao Tzu

R. L. WING

A DOLPHIN BOOK / DOUBLEDAY & COMPANY, INC.
Garden City, New York
1986

Design/Rita Aero
Research/Stephanie Rick
Calligraphy/Tse Leong Toy
Cover Calligraphy/Lam-po Leong
Caption Calligraphy/Johanna Yeung
Illustrations/Scott Bartlett

Library of Congress Cataloging in Publication Data
Wing, R.L.
The tao of power

"A Dolphin Book"
1. Lao-Tzu.   Tao te ching.   1. Lao-tzu.   Tao te ching.
English.   II. Title.
BL1900.L35W55   1986   299:51482

Library of Congress Catalog Card Number: 85-10210
ISBN: 0-385-19637-7
Copyright © 1986 by Immedia
All Rights Reserved
Printed in the United States of America

FIRST EDITION

CONTENTS

Notes on the Translation

THE TAO OF POWER IS A NEW TRANSLATION, from Chinese into English, of the twenty-five-hundred-year-old classic, the *Tao Te Ching* by Lao Tzu, a philosopher of the sixth century B.C. In this translation, I have, whenever possible, followed the original Chinese text word for word, without adding rhyme or poetic phraseology. The original text, in Chinese script, appears in the book along with each translated passage so that those readers interested in this unusual and rather beautiful written language should be able to find their way through the Chinese script, even without prior knowledge of the characters.

Ancient Chinese is an obscure and paradoxical language. It has no active or passive voice, no singular or plural. Nearly every word can be used as any part of speech. The translator must make these distinctions for the reader, and choose the best possible case for the most accurate transmission of the intent of the work. I have used the plural case throughout because it seems to be the most universal way to state a philosophical premise, and I believe this best reflects the spirit of the work.

To offset the terseness of the translation and clarify its meaning, the lines of the passages have been typographically arranged on the page to suggest the feeling and rhythm of the original. Ancient Chinese texts have no punctuation, and it is again the translator's role to separate the ideas in a way that makes them accessible to the reader. Although the eighty-one passages are untitled, I have given each one a title that hints at the concept conveyed within. Traditionally, the *Tao Te Ching* is divided into two parts, with passage No. 38 beginning the second section.

I did not translate the word *Tao* (pronounced *dow* as in *dowel*) since it is a concept that is increasingly familiar to Western readers. Although it is often translated as "the Way," this term does not accurately express the true meaning of *Tao*, which is, to be precise, "the Way the universe works." In any event, the *Tao Te Ching* is dedicated to defining *Tao*, so there is no real need for an English translation of the word. The word *Te* (pronounced *der* as in *order*) is frequently translated as "virtue," which is an unfortunate word choice for a very important concept. In the West, virtue suggests righteousness, but in fact *Te* is a term that refers to the potential energy that comes from being in the right place and in the right frame of mind at the right time. The early Chinese regarded the planting of seeds as *Te*, and *Te* came to mean stored energy or potentiality, and sometimes magic power. Not until the widespread popularity of Confucian ideals centuries later, did *Te* begin to take on the meaning of socially imposed moral conduct, and this was eventually translated into English as "virtue." Therefore, following the lead of a number of other modern translators, I have returned the meaning of *Te* to its original concept, "Power."

I have made very few transpositions — substitutions of modern terminology for archaic expressions — and where they do occur, they are footnoted in the text. One such substitution throughout is the term *sheng jen*, which means "holy man" or "sage." I felt the meaning of this term was best served with the words "Evolved Individual." Another transposition is the Chinese word *kuo*, which can be translated as "kingdom" or "government." In this case, I chose to use the word "organization" since *kuo*, in a universal sense, may refer to any social organization.

In trying to understand a work like the *Tao Te Ching*, it is important to keep in mind that Chinese characters are not so much representations of words as they are symbols for ideas. Lao Tzu is showing us in symbols, not telling us in words, what he thinks. Therefore, the work is meant to be transmitted mind to mind, while the words are incidental to the central idea. Because of its idea-embedded nature, the *Tao Te Ching* is a work that brings truth to the adage: It is better to read one book one hundred times than one hundred books one time.

The eighty-one passages are stark, vivid, and sometimes haunting. They are filled with metaphor and paradox. The *Tao Te Ching* is really intended to be a catalyst for the mind of the reader, triggering insights into the nature of reality — and, in turn, the reader must participate in creating meaning in the work. Lao Tzu did not try to make the work finite or exacting, for then it would not mutate through time; it would not act like the *Tao*. Certainly, in this, he achieved his aim.

To aid the reader in understanding Lao Tzu's work, I have added commentaries adjacent to each of the translated passages. These commentaries provide an explanation of the allusive concepts contained in the passages, and they may serve as departure points for the reader's own contemplations. I cannot pretend to see the world the way that Lao Tzu did in the sixth century B.C.; therefore, in my commentaries I have attempted to sift through the time that separates us, looking for the universal connections between then and now, reaching across the semantic and cosmological gulf into early Taoist speculations about the nature of the universe.

I am not the first who has attempted to bridge this gulf, and certainly I will not be the last. The *Tao Te Ching* periodically compels readers and translators to usher it along through time. And, in turn, the book brings with it, into its new form, an illumination that is at once startling and gratifying. I believe the experience was most eloquently described by one English translator of the *Tao Te Ching*, Dr. Lionel Giles, Keeper of the Oriental Manuscripts at the British Museum. He made the following comments in 1937:

Never, surely, has so much thought been compressed into so small a space. Throughout the universe there are scattered a certain number of stars belonging to a class known as "white dwarfs." They are usually very small, yet the atoms of which they consist are crushed together so closely that their weight is enormous in relation to their size, and this entails the radiation of so much energy that the surface is kept at a temperature vastly hotter than that of the sun. The *Tao Te Ching* may fitly be called a "white dwarf" of philosophical literature, so weighty is it, so compact, and so suggestive of a mind radiating thought at white heat.

R. L. Wing
San Francisco, 1986

THE TAO

NO ONE ACTUALLY KNOWS where the *Tao Te Ching* came from, but this slim book of about five thousand words forms the foundation of classical Chinese philosophy. Simply stated, the book explains an evolving force called *Tao* that operates throughout the universe; and it describes the personal power that comes from being in step with the *Tao*, which is known as *Te*. The word *Ching* means "classic."

Throughout the twenty-five-hundred-year history of the *Tao Te Ching,* hundreds of translations and commentaries have been published — more than fifty in English alone — making it, next to the Bible, the world's most-translated classic. The book has found an audience in each new generation and never seems to lose its provocative intellectual value. In this decade, the *Tao Te Ching* has been rediscovered by physicists, who find in it remarkable correlations with their theories of the universe. The *Tao Te Ching*, moreover, is being explored by psychologists and business leaders who hope to understand that quality of the oriental mind that makes it so centered and insightful in world affairs and economics. The book casts a spell over those who contemplate it; it is a magnet for minds with the potential to influence society. Indeed, influencing society is what the *Tao Te Ching* is all about.

According to legend, the book was written by Lao Tzu, a gifted scholar who lived nearly twenty-six centuries ago and worked as the Custodian of the Imperial Archives during the reign of the Chou Dynasty. Lao Tzu experienced a time of political unrest not unlike our own. His world was divided into hundreds of separate provinces, each with its own laws and leaders. He saw a buildup of arms and hostilities as each province competed for political supremacy. Every aggressive act was met with further hostility and aggression, until it seemed to the war-torn people of China that they stood on the threshold of complete destruction and that their world would finish as a wasteland.

Sensing the hopelessness of the era, with its hostile political counter-reactions spiraling out of control, Lao Tzu retired from his position and prepared to leave the civilized world forever. Before he was allowed to pass through the gates of the capital into the mountains beyond, Yin Hsi, Keeper of the Gate, insisted that Lao Tzu write down what he knew for the enlightenment of those left behind. Lao Tzu crafted the *Tao Te Ching*, directing it toward those individuals who were in a position to guide others — toward princes and politicians, employers and educators.

What Lao Tzu tells leaders is essentially this: Discover who you are. Learn to sense the world around you directly, and contemplate your impressions deeply. Do not rely on ideologies, because to do so will rob your life of meaning and make you unfit to lead. Cultivate and make trustworthy your intuition, because a leader who is not intuitive cannot predict change. Build up your personal power (*Te*) though your awareness and knowledge of the physical laws as they operate both in the universe and in the minds of others (*Tao*) — then use that power to direct events, without resorting to force. How is this done? Use attitude instead of action, and lead others by guiding rather than ruling. Manage people by letting them act on you, and not the other way around. In this way, your subjects will develop a sense of self-government, and you, as their guide, will be rewarded with their loyalty and cooperation. Learn to achieve your ends without means, by cultivating a strong vision of the way things must naturally resolve themselves. Practice simplicity. Continue to grow.

Lao Tzu believed that the ideal way to direct events was to use methods that do not create resistance or elicit counter-reactions. In observing the laws of nature, he realized that excessive force in a particular direction tends to trigger the growth of an opposing force, and that therefore the use of force cannot be the basis for establishing a strong and lasting social foundation. Lao Tzu believed that it was essential for leaders to be ever observant of the laws of nature — in short, to develop a sophisticated understanding of the ways that matter and energy function in the universe. He called this *Tao*. He realized that the physical laws of the universe directly affect the ways that individuals tend to behave and societies tend to evolve, and that to comprehend these laws could give a leader the power (*Te*) to bring harmony to the world.

The *Tao Te Ching* is a challenge. It challenges us to see the world as it actually is by accepting the stark truth of the physical laws that control existence and evolution. It challenges us to discover intellectual independence — a state of mind in which we have complete trust in our own perceptions of the world and can rely fully on the appropriateness of our own inspirations and instincts. It challenges us to find the courage to reject force, and instead, to influence others through our example, using nature as our pattern — balancing the extremes in the world instead of causing them. This final challenge is perhaps more vital today than ever before, both for ourselves and for our leaders. Lao Tzu put it this way:

> Evolved Individuals hold to the Tao,
> And regard the world as their Pattern.
>
> They do not display themselves;
>   Therefore they are illuminated.
> They do not define themselves;
>   Therefore they are distinguished.
> They do not make claims;
>   Therefore they are credited.
> They do not boast;
>   Therefore they advance.

THE TAO OF POWER

THE *TAO TE CHING* EXPLORES A REMARKABLE POWER that is latent in every individual. This power, which Lao Tzu calls *Te,* emerges when one is aware of and aligned with the forces in nature (*Tao*). It is essential to Lao Tzu's system that we understand why and how reality functions, and that we come to realize that nature invariably takes its course. We already know that it is rarely worth the effort to swim upstream, but do we know which way the stream is flowing? We realize that it is difficult and unsatisfying to cut across the grain, but can we see which way the grain runs? Lao Tzu believed that a constant awareness of the patterns in nature will bring us insights into the parallel patterns in human behavior: Just as spring follows winter in nature, growth follows repression in society; just as too much gravity will collapse a star, too much possessiveness will collapse an idea.

Like all matter and energy in the universe, the emotional and intellectual structures that we build are constantly transformed by outside forces. Much of our power is wasted in propping up our beliefs, defending them, and convincing others to believe in them so that they might become "permanent." Once we understand the folly in this, we gain power by using the evolution in nature to our advantage — accepting, incorporating, and supporting change when and where it wants to occur. Our cooperation with the forces in nature makes us a part of those forces. Our decisions become astute because they are based on a dynamic, evolving reality, not on fixed or wishful thinking. We are able to see things that others might not because the reach of our minds is extended through the contemplation of the universe. We develop vision and we help create the future with the power of our vision.

Lao Tzu believed that when people do not have a sense of power they become resentful and uncooperative. Individuals who do not feel personal power feel fear. They fear the unknown because they do not identify with the world outside of themselves; thus their psychic integration is severely damaged and they are a danger to their society. Tyrants do not feel power, they feel frustration and impotency. They wield force, but it is a form of aggression, not authority. On closer inspection, it becomes apparent that individuals who dominate others are, in fact, enslaved by insecurity and are slowly and mysteriously hurt by their own actions. Lao Tzu attributed most of the world's ills to the fact that people do not feel powerful and independent.

Powerful individuals never show their strength, yet others listen to them because they seem to *know*. They radiate knowledge, but it is an intuitive knowing that comes from a direct understanding and experience with the ways of nature. They are compassionate and generous because they instinctively realize that power continues to flow through them only when they pass it on. Like electricity, the more energy, inspiration, and information they conduct, the more they receive.

True power is the ability to influence and change the world while living a simple, intelligent, and experientially rich existence. Powerful individuals influence others with the force of example and attitude. Within groups, they have great presence — intellectual gravity — that influences the minds of those exposed to them. Intellectual gravity develops as a result of expanded identification — an identification that reaches far outside the self. Individuals who can identify with the evolution of reality develop significance and power because the force of their awareness is actively defining the universe around them.

There are two major changes that occur in the lives of individuals who achieve personal power: the rise of intellectual independence and the need for simplicity. Taoism, as a way of understanding the universe, is not based on faith; it is based on experience. The human mind is evolving, while all social systems are temporary experiments. Relying on systems of understanding created or interpreted by others will dull the instincts and prevent individuals from cultivating and expanding their own minds. Power will not develop in individuals who allow doctrine and dogma to stand between them and direct personal knowledge of the universe.

Simplicity in conduct, in beliefs, and in environment brings an individual very close to the truth of reality. Individuals who practice simplicity cannot be used because they already have everything they need; they cannot be lied to because a lie merely reveals to them another aspect of reality. An attraction to simplicity is essentially an attraction to freedom — the highest expression of personal power. We are taught to think of freedom as something one has, but it is really the absence of things that brings freedom to the individual and meaning into life. To let go of things — unnecessary desires, superfluous possessions — is to have them. Lao Tzu believed that an individual life contains the whole universe, but when individuals develop fixations about certain parts of life they become narrow and shallow and uncentered. Fixations and desires create a crisis within the mind. As individuals let go of desires, feelings of freedom, security, independence, and power increase accordingly.

The *Tao Te Ching* has a self-selecting audience — it seems to attract individuals who are on the threshold of evolutionary intellectual growth. The philosophy presents an opportunity for psychological breakthrough — a breakthrough in attitude (because we must rethink our relationship with the universe) and a breakthrough in personal goals (because our desires become rooted in simplicity and we are freed of emotional delusion). Those who find a resonant voice in Lao Tzu are destined to transcend the commonplace and to use the power that comes from their personal freedom to shape the future.

The *Tao Te Ching* is written on many levels. There is a level waiting just below the one you currently understand. The deeper you penetrate, the more power you develop. The more potential you have for influence in the world, the stronger and more penetrating your insights become. The philosophy that Lao Tzu left behind is actually an experiment, one that individuals undertake when they are ready to enter the next phase of human evolution — that of fully conscious beings who are actively directing both their own destinies and the destiny of the world around them. In his ultimate vision, Lao Tzu believed that if each and every one of us could realize and gain control of our evolutionary power, it would invisibly unite us and allow us to become a collective, compassionate, and fully aware social and universal organism.

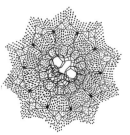

END VIEW OF A
DNA MOLECULE

THE TAO OF NATURE

LAO TZU WAS PERHAPS THE WORLD'S FIRST theoretical physicist. He devoted all of his intellectual energy to observing nature and its physical laws and to noting the interdependent relationship of all things. He saw a unified field of forces that he called *Tao*, but because what he saw could not be expressed in a logical, analytical fashion, he conveyed it through paradox. The eighty-one chapters in his small book are riddled with self-contradictory phrases: "The *Tao* illuminated appears to be obscure. The *Tao* advancing appears to be retreating. It is the form of the formless; the image of nothingness." Lao Tzu used paradox to provoke an unusual awareness in his readers, and to help explain the patterns and cycles, the parity and complementarity, that he saw superimposed on reality by the physical forces in the universe. The most striking of these patterns, central to the *Tao Te Ching*, is that of polarity.

Polarity arises from the Taoist view of the cosmological origins of the universe: Before existence there was an idea — an Absolute. The Chinese call it *T'ai Chi*, the Supreme Ultimate. The Absolute, in a sudden and tremendous desire to know itself, divided itself from nonexistence in a cataclysmic event resulting in endless cause and effect — an event that neatly parallels the so-called Big Bang Theory. Instantly, space was formed and time began, and two charged states came into being, *yin* (negative) and *yang* (positive). As a result of the complementary polarity of *yin* and *yang*, matter and energy, which were at first undifferentiated, separated and regrouped into the physical reality that became our universe.

Lao Tzu believed that everything that exists comes into reality through the polarity of *yin* and *yang*. He called the specific physical laws and cycles that control and govern reality the *Tao*, and suggested that the actions of the *Tao* reflect the purpose of a larger entity (the Absolute). So if reality came about because the Absolute wanted to know itself, then our evolutionary destiny must be to help it get a good look by investigating, observing, and emulating nature.

In the Taoist view, developing an awareness of the laws of nature, especially as they manifest themselves in human culture, is a major component of personal growth and evolution. Lao Tzu believed that people and their attitudes and actions are inseparable from the physical phenomena surrounding them; and that either might alter the reality of the other.

Since the advent of quantum mechanics (the mathematics that describes the interactions that take place at the sub-atomic level), scientists have become intrigued with the link between human awareness and the workings of the universe. Quantum mechanics seems to suggest that the sub-atomic world — and even the world beyond the atom — has no independent structure at all until defined by the human intellect. Werner Heisenberg, who transformed physics when he developed this concept in 1927, notes: "Natural science does not simply describe and explain nature; it is a part of the interplay between nature and ourselves.... What we observe is not nature itself, but nature exposed to our method of questioning." A new generation of physicists are now postulating that a universe cannot even come into existence unless it contains the possibility of life. They suggest that we live in a participatory universe where all reality and physical laws are dependent upon an observer to formulate them. Lao Tzu would clearly concur.

Conceiving of a universe where reality is shaped through the force of the intellect (and vice versa) may be somewhat easier for physicists than it is for the rest of us, but it is a concept that is indispensable to anyone seeking powerful insights into the ways of the world. All investigations — whether at the atomic level or at the level of our own cultural behavior — yield more refined and accurate information when approached from this paradoxical point of view. Fortunately, the structure of the brain and the bilateral processes of the mind can make effective use of this form of thought.

The brain accepts all types of information from all stimuli simultaneously, and the mind processes it in the form of emotional responses, intuitive feelings, and logically formulated analyses. In the West, we rely almost exclusively on logical analysis. We are encouraged to think in a linear fashion, using words and numbers to draw conclusions about our work and our lives. These logical functions, according to neurological research, are performed by the left hemisphere of the brain. At the same time, we learn to discount aesthetic or intuitive information — a right-hemisphere function — because it is considered less valuable to our culture. Thus we find ourselves primarily concerned with measuring events and analyzing their meaning, rather than creating and directing their flow. We are taught to ignore the intuitive or irrational, no matter how strong these "gut feelings" might be. As these right-hemisphere feelings are repressed, we lose touch with our intuitive mind and our insights become increasingly rare.

Lao Tzu believed that intuitive knowledge was the purest form of information. For that reason, he expressed his philosophy in the form of thought experiments — mental exercises designed to enhance and evolve the intuitive skills. In the *Tao Te Ching*, he compels us to use intuition as an equal partner with logic, and encourages us to combine our cognitive understanding of the world around us with a strong personal vision. Neurologically, we might call this a "whole-mind" approach, wherein the spatially and aesthetically astute right hemisphere of the brain is put into use along with the analytically and logically oriented left hemisphere. In this way, we gain a holistic and precise view of reality because we are also perceiving mood, change, and possibility — the mood of the times, the change as society evolves, and the possible future we might create. It is the view of the artist, the philosopher, the visionary — a view that has always carried with it the power to influence the world.

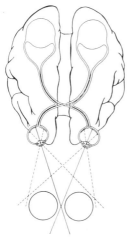

THE RIGHT MIND APPROACH

MANY OF THE PHILOSOPHICAL CLASSICS OF CHINA are written in a style for which there is no counterpart in Western literature. The majority of Western philosophy seems to emerge from the analytical left hemisphere of the brain, wherein a hypothesis is logically developed through a number of chapters until a conclusion is reached at the end of the book. Chinese classics, by contrast, seem to emerge from the spatially oriented right hemisphere of the brain. These works are, in a sense, holographic: each chapter is complete and each reflects the entire book. The only difference between chapters is a very slight shift in the angle of the view of the central premise. Thus, when exploring a classic like the *Tao Te Ching*, it may be appropriate to match its nonlinear style by reading the book at random.

When Eastern scholars explore a philosophical classic, they look for a subjective experience that might stimulate their intuitive understanding of the work. Perhaps they will open the book at random in order to select the next passage to contemplate. Using chance and synchronicity in their approach they can then contemplate, too, why that particular passage appeared in their lives at that particular moment.

In nature, a snowflake is a snowflake — until we take a closer look and see that no two snowflakes are formed in the same way. So too, in human nature, no two individuals are informed in the same way. Those who would like to allow nature to determine their intellectual path through the *Tao Te Ching* may find that a random approach to the text will help trigger the spirit of the moment and open their mind to self-discovery. Readers who are familiar with Chinese philosophy will recognize the approach that follows, since similar forms of subjective interaction are used in such classics as the *T'ai Hsuan Ching,* a philosophical work from the early history of China (c.1 B.C.), and the *I Ching*.

In the *I Ching*, each of the sixty-four passages is represented by a hexagram, a mathematical diagram constructed from six stacked lines of two types (solid and broken). There are sixty-four possible arrangements of these two types of lines (2^6). Through the use of the hexagrams, the Chinese developed the binary numbering system nearly three millennia before it reached the rest of the world. Their binary system was based on the the square of 8, thus sixty-four became an important number in Chinese philosophy.

It is no accident that the *Tao Te Ching* has eighty-one chapters, for eighty-one, the square of 9, is also a significant number to those Chinese philosophers who treasured the symmetry of numbers. The elegance of the number eighty-one was expressed by the ancient Chinese with the use of mathematical diagrams known as tetragrams. A tetragram is constructed from four stacked lines of three types (solid, broken, and twice-broken). There are eighty-one possible arrangements of these three types of lines (3^4). The tetragrams, which were once used to randomly explore the *T'ai Hsuan Ching*, are combined here with the eighty-one passages of the *Tao Te Ching*. They appear in the Tetragram Arrangement on the next page.

There are two ways to use the tetragrams to select one of the passages in the *Tao Te Ching*. The first method is quick and requires the use of a six-sided object — dice were invented by the Chinese for purposes such as this. The other

HEXAGRAM

TETRAGRAM

TETRAGRAM ARRANGEMENT

73	64	55	46	37	28	19	10	1
74	65	56	47	38	29	20	11	2
75	66	57	48	39	30	21	12	3
76	67	58	49	40	31	22	13	4
77	68	59	50	41	32	23	14	5
78	69	60	51	42	33	24	15	6
79	70	61	52	43	34	25	16	7
80	71	62	53	44	35	26	17	8
81	72	63	54	45	36	27	18	9

method, also traditional, involves the counting of sixty-four wooden sticks — usually the dried stems of the yarrow plant. This method takes several minutes to accomplish. Both methods are merely ways to generate a random number — to isolate a moment in time and space as a departure point for your own investigation into the *Tao Te Ching*. There is nothing significant about this process in itself.

To use the dice method, you will need a single die and a pencil and paper. The first roll of the die represents the bottom line of the tetragram. Read the die as shown below and draw the corresponding line. Now, repeat this process three more times until you have constructed, **from the bottom up**, a complete tetragram.

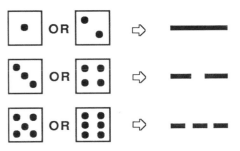

To use the stick counting method, you will need to find sixty-four long (6 to 12 inches) thin sticks. Once you gather your sticks, you will need a surface to work on and a pencil and paper.

1. Separate the sticks at random into three bundles in front of you.

2. Pick up the bundle on the far right and count it out by threes. There will be either 0, 1, or 2 sticks remaining. Put the remainder to one side. **If the remainder is 0, take one stick from the bundle you just counted and put that aside instead.**

3. Repeat step 2 for the middle bundle, then add the remainder to the remainder from the first bundle.

4. Repeat step 2 for the final bundle and add the remainder to the remainder of the first two bundles.

5. Total the number of sticks in the remainder pile. There will be 3, 4, or 5. This number represents the bottom line of your tetragram. Refer to the diagram below and draw the corresponding line.

6. Gather all the sticks and repeat this entire process three more times, beginning with step 1, until you have built, **from the bottom up**, a tetragram.

$$3 \Rightarrow \rule{2cm}{2mm}$$

$$4 \Rightarrow \rule{0.8cm}{2mm}\ \ \rule{0.8cm}{2mm}$$

$$5 \Rightarrow \rule{0.5cm}{2mm}\ \rule{0.5cm}{2mm}\ \rule{0.5cm}{2mm}$$

To determine the number of your tetragram, refer to the Bigram Chart on the next page. Since the tetragram is constructed from the bottom up, the two lower lines are called the lower bigram, and the two upper lines are called the upper bigram. Divide your tetragram into bigrams, then look down the right hand column and locate your lower bigram. Now, trace horizontally across that column until you are directly under your upper bigram. The number you will find there corresponds to the number of one of the passages in the *Tao Te Ching*. This, then, is the passage you will read next, for it is the next step in your journey through *The Tao of Power*. You may wish to use some of the Journal pages in the book to keep track of the sequence of your travels.

BIGRAM CHART

To locate a tetragram on the Bigram Chart, divide the tetragram you receive into two bigrams, upper and lower, as shown in the example below. Next locate the upper bigram across the top of the Chart. Then find the lower bigram on the right side of the Chart and trace across that row until you are under the upper bigram. The number you find there corresponds to one of the passages in *The Tao of Power*.

35 = UPPER BIGRAM / LOWER BIGRAM

81	80	79	78	77	76	75	74	73
72	71	70	69	68	67	66	65	64
63	62	61	60	59	58	57	56	55
54	53	52	51	50	49	48	47	46
45	44	43	42	41	40	39	38	37
36	35	34	33	32	31	30	29	28
27	26	25	24	23	22	21	20	19
18	17	16	15	14	13	12	11	10
9	8	7	6	5	4	3	2	1

△ UPPER BIGRAM
▽ LOWER BIGRAM

THE LEFT MIND APPROACH

THE RIGHT HEMISPHERE OF THE BRAIN attempts to understand what it experiences through overall intuitive impressions. It tries to encompass, in its impressions, all of the changing details of an event, even though it cannot analyze the way they actually fit together to form a whole. This hemisphere is more involved in gaining a broad understanding than it is in examining the details. It takes a top-down approach from an orbiting perspective.

The left hemisphere, by comparison, understands what it experiences by measuring, analyzing, and categorizing each detail of an event. It learns about the forest by examining each tree; and over time it builds, from the bottom up, an understanding. For this reason, the left hemisphere lends itself to a more formal exploration of the *Tao Te Ching* than does the right hemisphere.

Because each passage in the book describes a different intellectual or behavioral interaction with the *Tao*, each passage explores a specific aspect of potential power (*Te*). To explore these power topics in detail, the eighty-one passages of the *Tao Te Ching* can be divided into six separate sections. The interpretations in any of the six sections, when read contiguously, examine a specific theme throughout that section. Therefore, six distinct approaches to power will be investigated in this arrangement of the passages. The Guide to the Passages, on the next page, will help you locate the power area that you would like to investigate. They are:

POWER IN NATURE: Each of these passages focuses on the very basic physical laws that describe Taoist philosophy. This section deals with the cosmology of the Tao and the origins of the universe and is best understood by using a scientific point of view.

POWER IN AWARENESS: These passages further explore the physical laws operating in nature as well as the basic philosophical assumptions in Taoism. The information in this section is presented in the form of thought experiments: awareness exercises that can be used to expand the mind and cultivate the powers of intuition.

POWER IN PROJECTION: These passages comprise another set of thought or idea experiments. In this section, however, the exercises are designed to help individuals use attitude and conduct in order to cultivate personal power and gain influence within their environment.

POWER IN LEADERSHIP: The passages in this section are aimed directly at those who are in positions of leadership. Each passage describes the ideal relationship between leaders and their subjects, revealing the most effective methods for managing others and accomplishing aims.

POWER IN ORGANIZATIONS: This section examines the behavior of individuals engaged in group endeavors, as well as the conduct of organizations involved in worldly endeavors. These passages describe those Taoist principles that lead to the harmonious achievement of group objectives.

POWER IN NONINTERFERENCE: Although the principle of tactical noninterference (Lao Tzu calls it *wu wei*, or nonaction) is touched upon in many of the passages in the *Tao Te Ching*, the passages selected for this section explore in detail the use of "hands-off" techniques for achieving lasting influence in worldly endeavors.

GUIDE TO THE PASSAGES

THE WHOLE MIND APPROACH

WHEN INDIVIDUALS USE THEIR WHOLE MIND to understand and interact with the world around them, they are, in a sense, using two distinct minds. Their *worldly mind* allows them to formulate logical reactions to the physical reality in their environment, while their *universal mind* collects and responds to impressions of both physical and nonphysical reality. The fact is, all of us experience reality and accumulate information with both minds simultaneously, but not all of us take full advantage of this expanded awareness.

The worldly mind focuses on the plane of physical reality. Physical reality is a body of information that is experienced through the physical senses: sight, sound, and touch. This information is processed by the mind in a contained, analytical fashion, using primarily the language of words and numbers to achieve the stability of logic. Some individuals live their entire lives and base all of their experiences on information found on this plane, but it is really a world more suited to machines than people.

The universal mind works on the plane of physical reality but focuses, also, on nonphysical reality. Nonphysical reality is a body of information that is experienced with a second set of senses that includes instinct and intuition. This information is processed by the mind in a universal, open-ended fashion, using the language of pattern to achieve the advantage of insight.

The goal of Taoist philosophy is to combine these two minds into a working perspective. This is clearly a timely contribution to the West, where we are predisposed to information that comes solely from the physical plane. Indeed, the physical plane can be touched, heard, and seen — and therefore, it is real. When we act on it, it changes; and this is immediately gratifying and, certainly, intellectually safe. But herein lies a principal paradox in Taoist philosophy.

If individuals do all of their thinking on the physical plane and make little effort on the nonphysical plane — cultivating intuition, gaining instinctive knowledge of the workings of the universe, and developing the insight to evolve both themselves and their society — then those lives have no real meaning or significance in terms of physical reality. This is so because work done on the nonphysical plane is more aligned with the purpose of the universe and, therefore, it has a more powerful effect upon our physical reality. Our inner work influences and evolves the universe, which in turn, evolves our reality. So the deeper we work, the more striking the changes on the physical plane and the more rapid the evolution of the species as a whole. By comparison, our efforts on the physical surface of this remote piece of earth stranded in the farthest edge of the universe are not only insignificant, but hopelessly entangled in cause and effect, in action and reaction.

If we extend the Taoist ideal of a cooperative world-consciousness to universal dimensions, then the universe has but one purpose and evolution moves in one direction: toward the development of a vast network of a nervous system that will bring into existence a conscious mind for the entire universe. We, as individuals, and even as a world society, are then merely neurons in the growth of what, at the moment, is a very primitive, universal brain. We can see the embedded pattern of this growth reflected, for example, in the evolution of our species — from the simplest brain stem of the lower life forms to the complex brain-mind of humans; and we can see it in the evolution of our thinking tools — from the primitive computer that can calculate numbers to the interconnected network of an informed and discerning data structure.

The fact is, each of us knows far more about reality — past, present, and future — than we are able to understand and express rationally. And, whether or not we work on our inner development, we all experience, with our intuitive minds, the most profound truths about our world and our destiny. What we must do, then, is use our analytical, logical mind to bring this potentially vital information to the surface, where we can use it.

Throughout the book you will find Journal pages that can be useful in stimulating your insights into reality. To use them, you would record an experience in life, and then look for a pattern in that experience that correlates to larger physical patterns in the universe. The idea, here, is to translate your experiences all the way from the subjective and worldly to the objective and universal. All experiences in life, when intellectually evolved in this way, become "larger-than-personal" experiences and take on deeper meaning. Patterns emerge; periodically they repeat themselves. The act of describing your life in universal terms trains the mind to recognize these patterns, and by recognizing the natural cycle of events, you will begin to apprehend the future.

To use the Journal, select a lined page from the book and use it to describe an event, transaction, relationship, or revelation that seems to stand out on your path through life. Then pull your mind back from the details of the situation you just described and attempt to describe it again, using a metaphor from nature. For example, a dead-end position that forced you to change careers might find an analogy in a river pouring into a box canyon and eventually overflowing to form a new waterway. Or the difficulty encountered in launching a complex idea, which later becomes a popular product, might be described as the energy spent overcoming the inertia of a heavy object, and the subsequent momentum that propels it on. When a relationship is pulled apart by outside influences, we might compare it to a planet with limited mass whose satellite spins out of orbit. Or perhaps it is a heavy atom whose weakening nucleus jettisons an electron requiring a stronger charge.

When we record and retranslate our personal experiences in the language of nature, we are developing a dialogue with the universe. We begin to reidentify ourselves in the world, using our growing awareness of the cycles in nature: difficult and easy, blocked and open, positive and negative. Through our awareness of the physical laws as they are reflected in our lives, we form a direct and interdependent relationship with an elegant, impartial, and evolving universe. When we align our lives to the rhythms of this universe, we begin to understand its purpose and we begin to reflect its significance in our own lives.

The power and astuteness that we gain from this universal perspective can be applied to any of life's situations. We learn how people tend to behave and societies tend to evolve, and we recognize situations that hold no promise because they are structured in a way that will cause their own downfall. Thus we develop the power to direct our lives into a future that we, in fact, participate in creating. And, in doing so, we achieve the fulfillment that comes from leaving what we touch with our minds a little more evolved than we found it.

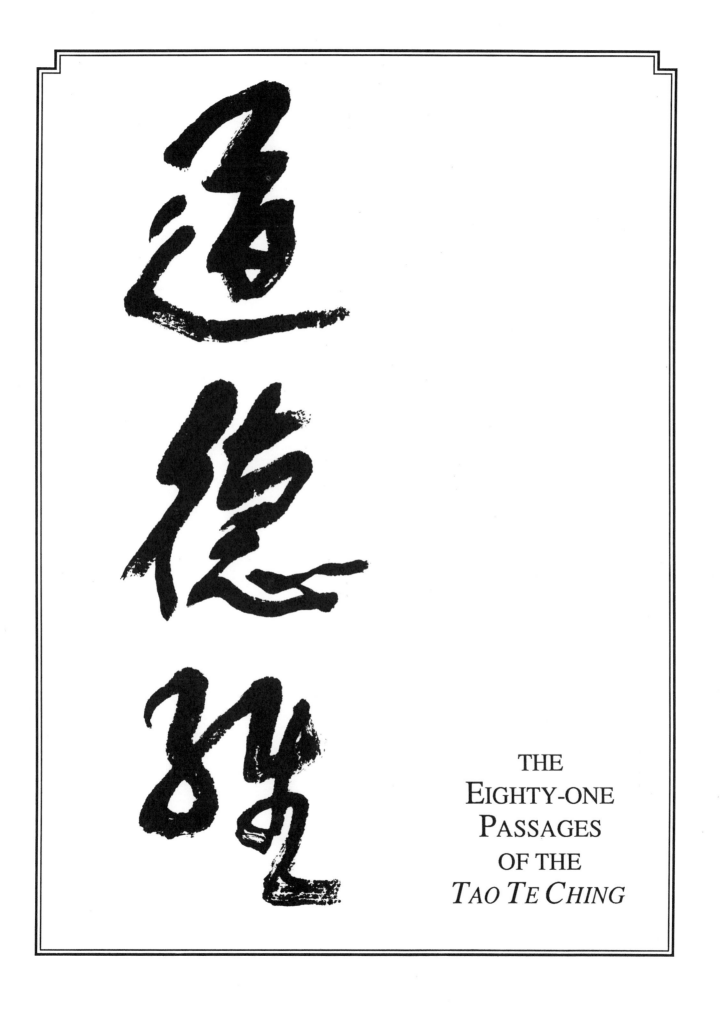

THE
EIGHTY-ONE
PASSAGES
OF THE
TAO TE CHING

ABSOLUTE

The character for absolute *or eternal (常) consists of a roof (宀), which divides
wind and rain (⺌), and has come to mean that which is superior. Under the roof
is a window (口) from which a piece of cloth (冂) is suspended (｜). The image
of the hanging cloth represents a flag or banner that flies constantly.*

THE BEGINNING OF POWER

The Tao that can be expressed
    Is not the Tao of the Absolute.
The name that can be named
    Is not the name of the Absolute.

The nameless originated Heaven and Earth.
The named is the Mother of All Things.

Thus, without expectation,
    One will always perceive the subtlety;
And, with expectation,
    One will always perceive the boundary.

The source of these two is identical,
Yet their names are different.
Together they are called profound,
Profound and mysterious,
The gateway to the Collective Subtlety.

Lao Tzu is at his most mysterious and obscure in this passage and, although it embodies many of the major elements of the philosophy of the *Tao Te Ching*, these elements are presented in more depth in other passages. Briefly, in the Taoist cosmology, the Absolute (the nameless) created a universe composed of matter and energy. The Tao (the named) is the behavior of the physical laws that coalesce matter and energy into All Things in the universe and direct their evolution.

In this passage and throughout the book, Lao Tzu urges his readers to drop their expectations, to discard their preconceived ideas, to abandon any method of knowing that might limit their horizons. When expectations are dropped, the mind expands, and reality expands along with the mind. Rather than merely perceiving where things are and where they have been (the boundary), an individual can begin to perceive the direction in which things are going (the subtlety). There is obvious power in apprehending the probabilities of the future, but moreover, a subtler power develops — one that brings insight and centeredness. Individuals begin to sense their potential ability to direct events with the force of their minds. They have located the path of personal power — "The gateway to the Collective Subtlety."

此兩者。同出而異名。同謂之玄。玄之又玄。眾妙之門

故常無欲。以觀其妙。常有欲。以觀其徼

道可道。非常道。名可名。非常名　無名天地之始。有名萬物之母

USING POLARITY

When all the world knows beauty as beauty,
    There is ugliness.
When they know good as good,
    There there is evil.

In this way
    Existence and nonexistence produce each other.
    Difficult and easy complete each other.
    Long and short contrast each other.
    High and low attract each other.
    Pitch and tone harmonize each other.
    Future and past follow each other.

Therefore, Evolved Individuals
    Hold their position without effort,
    Practice their philosophy without words,
    Are a part of All Things and overlook nothing.
    They produce but do not possess,
    Act without expectation,
    Succeed without taking credit.

Since, indeed, they take no credit, it remains with them.

The underlying principle in Taoist philosophy — just as in the physical sciences — is that of complementarity or polarity. Every action has its complementary reaction, and every pole is matched by one of opposite charge. The intellectual goal of the Taoist, then, is to find a correlation between the way matter and energy behave in nature and the ways that humans conduct themselves in societies.

Evolved Individuals use their awareness and understanding of the physical laws to shape events in their world. They know that nothing exists without the presence of its opposite; therefore they control their environment by avoiding extremes, even in a direction that might be considered "good." They do not preach their philosophy. They overlook nothing in their environment, and yet they do not try to possess things, not even their own ideas and work. They do not shoulder the burden of great expectations, and especially do not take credit for their achievements. As a result, nature and society are forced to balance toward them by bestowing credit on them.

天下皆知美之爲美。斯惡已。

皆知善之爲善。斯不善已

故有無相生。難易相成。長短相形。

高下相傾。音聲相和。前後相隨

是以聖人處無爲之事。行不言之教。萬物作焉而不辭。

生而不有。爲而不恃。功成而弗居 夫唯弗居是以不去

KEEPING PEACE

Do not exalt the very gifted,
    And people will not contend.
Do not treasure goods that are hard to get,
    And people will not become thieves.
Do not focus on desires,
    And people's minds will not be confused.

Therefore, Evolved Individuals lead others by
    Opening their minds,
    Reinforcing their centers,
    Relaxing their desires,
    Strengthening their characters.

Let the people always act without strategy or desire;
    Let the clever not venture to act.
Act without action,
    And nothing is without order.

Evolved Leaders know that their attitudes ultimately have greater influence than their actions. They know that those things that they respect and value soon become the motivating force behind their people. Therefore, they openly value worthwhile qualities that everyone can achieve — integrity, flexibility, and spontaneity. They do not emphasize extraordinary achievements or impressive possessions because they know this will undermine the harmony and accord among the people. Evolved Leaders bring peace and progress to their organization through the force of correct attitude. They practice noninterference and shape events with the power of their attitudes.

3

不尚賢。使民不爭。不貴難得之貨。

使民不爲盜。不見可欲。使民心不亂

是以聖人之治。虛其心。實其腹。

弱其志。強其骨

常使民無知無欲。使夫智者不敢爲也。

爲無爲。則無不治

TAO

The character for tao (道) is composed of several ideograms. The square with two horizontal dashes inside it represents a head with little tufts of hair (⌄) on top, the head of a leader (首). It is combined with the marks of feet running (彳) and stopping (止), which is now written in modernized script (辶), and means "to advance." Together they symbolize the higher mind, along with the feet, advancing on the same path.

THE NATURE OF THE TAO

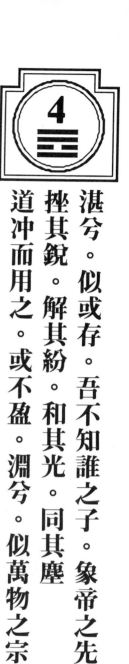

The Tao is empty and yet useful;
Somehow it never fills up.
So profound!
It resembles the source of All Things.

It blunts the sharpness,
Unties the tangles,
And harmonizes the brightness.
It identifies with the ways of the world.

So deep!
It resembles a certain existence.
I do not know whose offspring it is,
This Image in front of the source.

As Lao Tzu points out in this passage, the Tao is not the source of the universe —
the Absolute — but rather it is the way that everything in the universe changes and
evolves. Like a mathematical formula, the Tao is both empty and useful; and like a
formula, it can be used again and again. The Tao permeates nature. It moves through
the world, leveling the extremes — smoothing and harmonizing — and evolving the
universe and All Things in it.

The term *All Things* can be literally translated as "ten thousand
things." This is a symbolic number used to represent the entire
material universe.

HEAVEN AND EARTH

Three ideograms compose the character for heaven (天). *The splayed strokes at the bottom* (人) *represent a human walking. To show greatness, the arms are spread* (一). *Above the shoulders stretches the mantle of the cosmos* (⌐). Earth (地) *is depicted by horizontal lines symbolizing bedrock and soil* (二) *from which a growing thing sprouts* (丨). *Combined with the ancient symbol for a drinking vessel or horn* (卪), *which is now written in a modernized form* (也), *it implies the realm of humans.*

HOLDING TO THE CENTER

Heaven and Earth are impartial;
    They regard All Things as straw dogs.
 Evolved Individuals are impartial;
    They regard all people as straw dogs.

Between Heaven and Earth,
    The space is like a bellows.
The shape changes,
    But not the form.
The more it moves,
    The more it produces.

Too much talk will exhaust itself.
It is better to remain centered.

The concept of "Heaven and Earth" refers to the nonphysical and physical realms that reflect the actions of the Tao in worldly affairs. Because the Tao acts impartially in nature, Evolved Individuals do so as well. They know they must regard humankind impartially if they are to gain perspective about themselves and their own position in the world. Evolved Individuals, nevertheless, are compassionate in their emotional and intellectual independence. Because they are centered, they spontaneously react with benevolence. To hold to the center is to listen to the voice of the inner mind — an extension of the mind of the universe. To follow one is to be in harmony with the other. This is the path to self-discovery.

The term *impartial* can be literally translated as "not humane." The word *humane* is etymologically derived from two characters, "man" and "two" (signifying a group), and refers to people in identification with their society.

The term *straw dogs* comes from an ancient Chinese custom wherein animals were fashioned in straw to be burned in sacrificial rites. There was no emotional attachment to these images; they simply performed a cultural function.

多言數窮。不如守中

天地之間。其猶橐籥乎。虛而不屈。動而愈出

天地不仁。以萬物爲芻狗。聖人不仁。以百姓爲芻狗

VALLEY

The modern character for valley (谷) *is derived from an ancient and quite descriptive pictogram (
). It shows two mountains at the mouth of a deep gorge (
) with flowing waters (廿) below.*

PERCEIVING THE SUBTLE

The mystery of the valley is immortal;
    It is known as the Subtle Female.
The gateway of the Subtle Female
    Is the source of Heaven and Earth.

Everlasting, endless, it appears to exist.
Its usefulness comes with no effort.

In this passage, Lao Tzu refers to the Tao as the Subtle Female because the Tao reflects characteristics that Lao Tzu viewed as archetypically feminine. The Tao is passive, receptive, and tranquil — and yet the key to its mysterious power lies in its subtle behavior. Lao Tzu uses the image of the valley as a metaphor for the human perception of reality. The boundaries of the valley obscure the view of the source of creation beyond: the Absolute. The "gateway" — the Tao — leads from the source of creation into the valley where its actions become visible in worldly affairs (Heaven and Earth). The last sentence in this passage reminds Evolved Individuals that when they are in step with the Tao in worldly affairs, their endeavors can be completed effortlessly.

綿綿若存。用之不勤

是謂玄牝。玄牝之門。是謂天地根

谷神不死。

FU HSI

The first of China's legendary emperors, Fu Hsi is believed to have lived between 2953 and 2838 B.C. He is credited with the invention of the calendar and the marriage contract, and was the creator of the stringed musical instrument. He also taught his people to hunt, fish, and cook, as well as to raise animals domestically.

Fu Hsi developed the eight trigrams, a sequence of lines illustrating cause-effect relationships, which he is said to have discovered in the patterns on the shell of a tortoise. The eight trigrams later became the basis for the I Ching. Fu Hsi recognized the roles of constancy and change in nature and applied them to the affairs of society, in effect creating one of history's first management systems.

The National Palace Museum, Taipei, Taiwan

THE POWER OF SELFLESSNESS

Heaven is eternal, the Earth everlasting.
They can be eternal and everlasting
Because they do not exist for themselves.
For that reason they can exist eternally.

Therefore, Evolved Individuals
    Put themselves last,
        And yet they are first.
    Put themselves outside,
        And yet they remain.

Is it not because they are without self-interest
That their interests succeed?

The path of those who follow the Tao seems contrary to common sense and ordinary expectation. Evolved Individuals know that the cyclic actions of the Tao will ultimately bring into the foreground that which is currently in the background. This natural change occurs without force or resistance and it therefore endures. Thus, careful positioning is the strategy of Evolved Individuals. By putting themselves last and outside, they are employing subtlety and tactical inertness to compel the social environment to counterbalance and bring them forward naturally.

Although it is true that in acting without self-interest, one's interests will be fulfilled, individuals who put self-interest last discover that their desires are transformed. As their awareness expands, they develop priorities that are aligned intelligently with both the current situation and with larger influences in the world. For this reason, as their aims are fulfilled, their environment evolves.

7

天長地久。天地所以能長且久者。以其不自生。故能長生

非以其無私邪。故能成其私？

是以聖人後其身。而身先。外其身。而身存

NOT CONTEND

The character for not (不) *is composed of the symbol for a bird flying up (个) and disappearing from sight into the sky (一). The character for* contend (爭) *comes from the image of two hands (彐) struggling for the same object (｜).*

NONCOMPETITIVE VALUES

The highest value is like water.

The value in water benefits All Things,
    And yet it does not contend.
It stays in places that others disdain,
    And therefore is close to the Tao.

The value in a dwelling is location.
The value in a mind is depth.
The value in relations is benevolence.
The value in words is sincerity.
The value in leadership is order.
The value in work is competence.
The value in effort is timeliness.

Since, indeed, they do not contend,
There is no resentment.

Water is a recurring image in the *Tao Te Ching*. It is used to describe the behavior of Evolved Individuals — those who spontaneously bring progress to situations without inviting resistance or resentment. Like water, Evolved Individuals do not compete to reach high places but, instead, hold to lower ones. This Taoist ideal runs counter to the common view that one must contend and struggle to achieve success.

    The values mentioned in this passage are values that can be attained only with a fully expanded perspective: To achieve location one must know the whole; to achieve depth one must realize its possibility; to achieve benevolence one must comprehend human nature; to achieve sincerity one must know inner truth; to achieve order one must know the entire structure; to achieve competence one must know the results of a perfectly executed task; to achieve timeliness one must hold in mind both the past and future. With such a breadth of awareness, contention is unnecessary, for the instincts and intuition that develop as a result lead unfailingly to fulfillment.

上善若水　水善利萬物。而不爭。處衆人之所惡。故幾於道

居善地。心善淵。與善仁。言善信。

正善治。事善能。動善時　夫唯不爭。故無尤

LAO TZU PASSING THE BARRIER

Lao Tzu lived during what historians refer to as the Warring States Period, a time when China was engaged in a bitter war with itself. According to legend, at the age of 160, Lao Tzu grew weary of his world and its unnecessary struggles toward what he believed was easy and natural to attain: peace and progress. So he withdrew from his position at the Chinese Imperial Capital at Loyang and travelled west with his ox through the Han Ku Pass.

Meanwhile, the Keeper of the Pass, Yin Hsi, had foreseen in the meteorological patterns that vital information would be coming that day. When Lao Tzu arrived, Yin Hsi would not let the well-known scholar pass until Lao Tzu wrote down all that he knew. Lao Tzu camped nearby and composed a five-thousand-character classic, the Tao Te Ching. *He gave it to Yin Hsi and continued on his way into the mountains west of China. He was never seen again.*

MOA Museum of Art, Atami, Japan

TRANSCENDING DECLINE

Holding to fullness
Is not as good as stopping in time.

Sharpness that probes
Cannot protect for long.

A house filled with riches
Cannot be defended.

Pride in wealth and position
Is overlooking one's collapse.

Withdrawing when success is achieved
Is the Tao in Nature.

After developing situations and achieving success, Evolved Individuals do not linger to experience the inevitable cycle of decline. They know that if they stop to identify with their accomplishments, their inner growth will end and their downfall will begin. Nothing is static in nature. All things that reach their full maturity — whether plants and animals or planets and stars — must necessarily decline. Therefore Evolved Individuals never stop growing and never accumulate social or material burdens to slow their progress. When their work is done, they move on to the next task. In this way, they develop greatness and power.

功成身退。天之道

金玉滿堂。莫之能守

持而盈之。不如其已

富貴而驕。自遺其咎

揣而梲之。不可長保

INFLUENCE

Influence (氣) *comes from the philosophical concept of* ch'i: *the energy or essence of life. It was originally depicted with a drawing of the sun (☉) along with the symbol for fire (火) making curling vapors (气) rise from the earth (氣). The more recent character now depicts steam (气) rising from boiling rice (米), the principal food in the Chinese diet.*

INNER HARMONY

In managing your instincts and embracing Oneness,
    Can you be undivided?
In focusing your Influence,
    Can you yield as a newborn child?
In clearing your insight,
    Can you become free of error?
In loving people and leading the organization,
    Can you take no action?
In opening and closing the gateway to nature,
    Can you not weaken?
In seeing clearly in all directions,
    Can you be without knowledge?

Produce things, cultivate things;
Produce but do not possess.
Act without expectation.
Advance without dominating.
These are called the Subtle Powers.

Those who follow the Tao strive to recognize and reconcile the extremes in human nature. On one side is aggressiveness and conscious motive; on the other is spontaneity and the need for social integration. They know that the power they develop through work on the inner mind can only be maintained by resolving this inner polarity. Evolved Individuals realize that all of their experiences in life are a reflection of their personal cultivation, so they work deeply. They learn to achieve their purpose and master their environment by remaining objective and open to all forms of information. They avoid aggressive action, and they transcend unworthy desires. Instead, they shape their environment and direct the future with the influence of their intellectual gravity. These are the Subtle Powers.

The word *Influence* comes from the Chinese word *ch'i*, which is variously translated as "breath" or "vital force." It denotes the psychophysiological power in a human being and is associated with the martial art, *tai ch'i*.

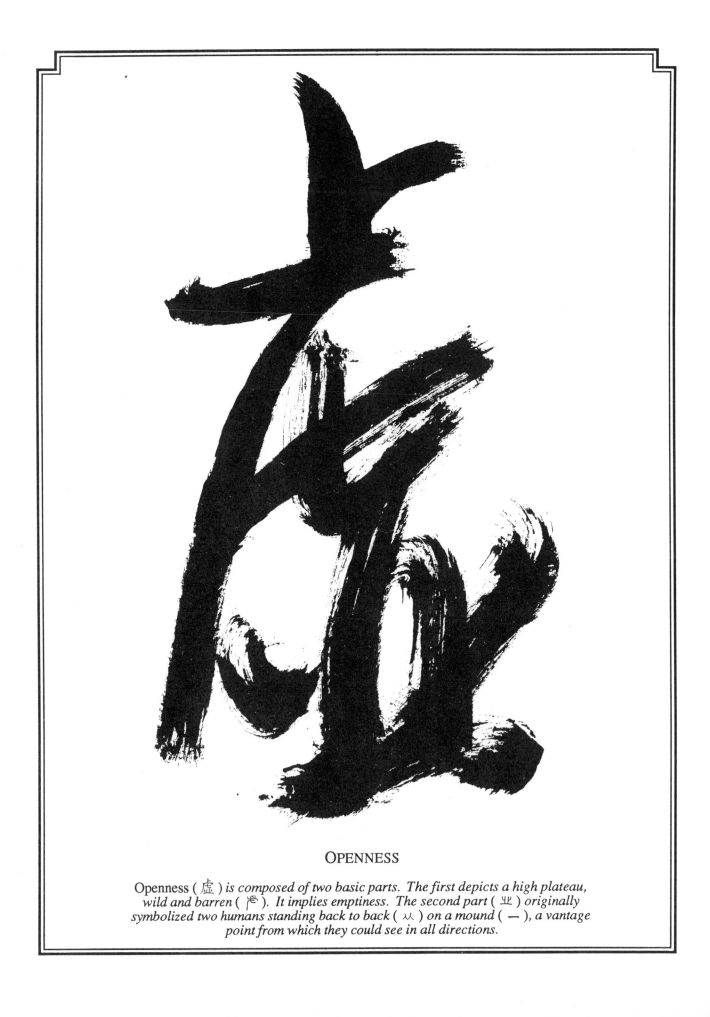

OPENNESS

Openness (虚) *is composed of two basic parts. The first depicts a high plateau, wild and barren (虍). It implies emptiness. The second part (业) originally symbolized two humans standing back to back (从) on a mound (—), a vantage point from which they could see in all directions.*

USING WHAT IS NOT

Thirty spokes converge at one hub;
    What is not there makes the wheel useful.
Clay is shaped to form a vessel;
    What is not there makes the vessel useful.
Doors and windows are cut to form a room;
    What is not there makes the room useful.

Therefore, take advantage of what is there,
By making use of what is not.

In natural events, the Tao is that vital component that is "not there," but which is indispensable to the process of change. In the same way that the missing electron causes atomic events, it is the Tao that inspires natural events. So, like physicists in their laboratories, Evolved Individuals know that it is possible to use what is not there to shape events in the outside world. To manifest an effect, they create a sense of absence that the natural forces are compelled to resolve. This intellectual integration with the laws of nature allows Evolved Individuals to position themselves effectively in the world.

故有之以爲利。無之以爲用

當其無有器之用。鑿戶牖以爲室。當其無有室之用

三十輻共一轂。當其無有車之用。埏埴以爲器。

THE YELLOW EMPEROR HUANG TI

Huang Ti, also known as the Yellow Emperor, is the most famous of the legendary rulers. He reigned from 2698 to 2598 B.C. and is credited with teaching his people to domesticate animals, as well as to cultivate crops. Huang Ti developed the earliest form of written Chinese, and, most important, he compiled the first Chinese medical guide, the Huang Ti Nei Ching.

Huang Ti related specific illnesses to the overall condition of the body and mind. He advised the practice of preventive medicine and the monitoring of the pulses. He believed that seven emotions, when either excessive or insufficient, can affect the body adversely. They are joy, anger, sadness, grief, pensiveness, fear, and fright. Still in use today, the Huang Ti Nei Ching *is considered the bible of Chinese medicine.*

The National Palace Museum, Taipei, Taiwan

CONTROLLING THE SENSES

The five colors will blind one's eye.
The five tones will deafen one's ear.
The five flavors will jade one's taste.

Racing and hunting will derange one's mind.
Goods that are hard to get will obstruct one's way.

Therefore, Evolved Individuals
Regard the center and not the eye.
Hence they discard one and receive the other.

Those who follow the Tao carefully control input to the senses in order to refine their insights and maintain an accurate perspective of the world. A cacophony of sounds, sights, and tastes, along with an accelerated, materially oriented life, will stand in the way of character development and inner clarity. Evolved Individuals know that intellectual independence and social freedom come through control of the senses. Wang Pi (c. 226-249), in one of the earliest commentaries on the *Tao Te Ching*, writes of this passage, "The center nourishes by receiving inward material things. The eye enslaves by directing one's attention outward to material things. Evolved Individuals, therefore, care little for the eye."

In order to reach into the "center" — to cultivate and hear the intuitive mind — Evolved Individuals limit their desires. When desires are under control, internal growth begins. Being free of the desire for superfluous possessions, free of the desire for praise or the fear of blame, results in great personal power. Those who have strong uncontrolled desires have limited possibilities in life; those who are attached to little experience all.

The word *center* comes from the Chinese character for "belly" and is generally interpreted as "that which is inside, the inner self."

五色令人目盲。五音令人耳聾。五味令人口爽

馳騁畋獵令人心發狂。難得之貨令人行妨

是以聖人。為腹不為目。故去彼取此

EXPANDING IDENTIFICATION

There is alarm in both favor and disgrace.
Esteem and fear are identified with the self.

What is the meaning of "alarm in both favor and disgrace?"
Favor ascends; disgrace descends.
To attain them brings alarm.
To lose them brings alarm.
That is the meaning of "alarm in both favor and disgrace."

What is the meaning of "esteem and fear are identified with the self?"
The reason for our fear
Is the presence of our self.
When we are selfless,
What is there to fear?

Therefore those who esteem the world as self
    Will be committed to the world.
Those who love the world as self
    Will be entrusted with the world.

Strong desires that are dependent on outside events or on the whims and judgments of others will lead individuals away from the cultivation of personal power. Lao Tzu suggests that both favor and disgrace force individuals into misdirected identification: identification with self. By limiting external dependencies and moving toward emotional independence, individuals reach a state where the intuition becomes finely tuned and the instincts can be trusted. This state inspires self-love and self-understanding. Individuals who master themselves become less egocentric, and their sense of identity begins to reach out into the world around them. Once they have attained this expanded awareness, they face a choice: They can identify with the world and its "favors and disgraces," and become committed to working in it; or they can love and accept it in all of its many forms. Evolved Individuals who love with compassion have the capacity to guide the world and direct its future.

若可寄天下。愛以身爲天下。若可託天下

及吾無身。吾有何患？故貴以身爲天下。

何謂貴大患若身？吾所以有大患者。爲吾有身。

寵爲上。寵爲下。得之若驚。失之若驚。是謂寵辱若驚

何謂寵辱若驚？

寵辱若驚。貴大患若身

THE ESSENCE OF TAO

Looked at but not seen:
    Its name is formless.
Listened to but not heard:
    Its name is soundless.
Reached for but not obtained:
    Its name is intangible.

These three cannot be analyzed,
So they mingle and act as one.

Its rising is not bright;
    Its setting is not dark.
Endlessly, the nameless goes on,
    Merging and returning to nothingness.

That is why it is called
    The form of the formless,
    The image of nothingness.
That is why it is called elusive.
    Confronted, its beginning is not seen.
    Followed, its end is not seen.

Hold on to the ancient Tao;
    Control the current reality.
Be aware of the ancient origins;
    This is called the Essence of Tao.

In this passage, one of the most mysterious in the *Tao Te Ching*, Lao Tzu hints at the nature of the Tao by describing what it is not. Awareness of the Tao cannot be reached through the senses: it cannot be seen, heard, or felt. It resides in the realm of the intuitive mind and can only be perceived through its effect in the environment: its effect on ideas, events, and social transformations. Worldly events occur in ever-repeating cycles, and those who follow the Tao learn to employ these cycles. They "hold on to the ancient Tao" by tracing events back to their very beginnings. At the same time, they trace back to the origins of their own existence in order to tap into the intuitive mind. With an intuitive understanding of the patterns in life, the outcome of events can be apprehended and reality can be altered. The Essence of the Tao is that an observer can evolve the observed through the act of tactical observation.

視之不見。名曰夷。聽之不聞。名曰希。搏之不得。名曰微

此三者不可致詰。故混而爲一

其上不皦。其下不昧。繩繩不可名。復歸於無物

是爲謂無狀之狀。

無物之象。是謂恍惚。迎之不見首。隨之不見後

執古之道。以御今之有。能知古始。是謂道紀

THE POWER IN SUBTLE FORCE

Those skillful in the ancient Tao
Are subtly ingenious and profoundly intuitive.
They are so deep they cannot be recognized.
Since, indeed, they cannot be recognized,
Their force can be contained.

So careful!
> As if wading a stream in winter.

So hesitant!
> As if respecting all sides in the community.

So reserved!
> As if acting as a guest.

So yielding!
> As if ice about to melt.

So candid!
> As if acting with simplicity.

So open!
> As if acting as a valley.

So integrated!
> As if acting as muddy water.

Who can harmonize with muddy water,
> And gradually arrive at clarity?

Who can move with stability,
> And gradually bring endurance to life?

Those who maintain the Tao
> Do not desire to become full.

Indeed, since they are not full,
> They can be used up and also renewed.

In this passage, Lao Tzu refers to reality as "muddy water," and suggests that in order to gain an insight into its unfolding pattern, one must be able to harmonize with its implicit unity and simplicity. Moreover, in order to use those insights to guide reality, one must move with a stability that causes no outside resistance. Evolved Individuals know that the less obvious they make their advantage, the more effective their power becomes. Thus, when using their power, Evolved Individuals are hesitant and reserved. They spend their power to bring clarity and cooperation into their world. They are candid, open, and integrated in their environment, and they serve as conduits, not as accumulators, for energy and matter. In this way, Evolved Individuals are ever replenished with the new and the vital as they continue to develop insight and power.

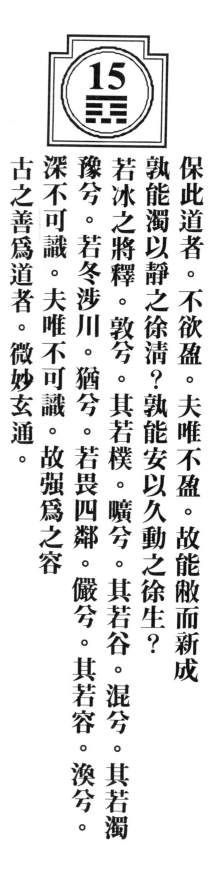

15

保此道者。不欲盈。夫唯不盈。故能敝而新成

孰能濁以靜之徐清？孰能安以久動之徐生？

若冰之將釋。敦兮。其若樸。曠兮。其若谷。混兮。其若濁

豫兮。若冬涉川。猶兮。若畏四鄰。儼兮。其若容。渙兮。

深不可識。夫唯不可識。故強為之容

古之善為道者。微妙玄通。

KNOWING THE ABSOLUTE

Attain the highest openness;
    Maintain the deepest harmony.
Become a part of All Things;
    In this way, I perceive the cycles.

Indeed, things are numerous;
    But each cycle merges with the source.
Merging with the source is called harmonizing;
    This is known as the cycle of destiny.

The cycle of destiny is called the Absolute;
    Knowing the Absolute is called insight.
To not know the Absolute
    Is to recklessly become a part of misfortune.

To know the Absolute is to be tolerant.
    What is tolerant becomes impartial;
    What is impartial becomes powerful;
    What is powerful becomes natural;
    What is natural becomes Tao.

What has Tao becomes everlasting
And free from harm throughout life.

In this passage, Lao Tzu describes the source of the Tao — the Absolute — and expresses his belief that one must contemplate the Absolute in order to fully comprehend the patterns of the Tao and the destiny of the universe in which it operates. This passage is an awareness exercise wherein the mind is fully expanded and placed in intimate identification with the universe and its reach for conciousness. Worldly expectations, desires, and fixations slip away and are replaced by receptivity, openness, and integration. In this way, those who follow the Tao touch the mind of the universe with their own. Thus they are able to apprehend the physical rhythms and cycles of the universe as they are reflected in the ways of society; they are able to predict the resolution of events and step out of the way of danger.

致虛極。守靜篤。萬物並作。吾以觀復

夫物芸芸。各復歸其根。

歸根曰靜。是謂復命

復命曰常。知常曰明。不知常。妄作凶

知常容。容乃公。公乃王。王乃天。天乃道

道乃久。沒身不殆

COLLECTIVE MIND

The character for collective *(衆) has two parts. In the first part, an eye (皿) takes in a group of humans (人) with a single glance, symbolizing a gathering. The second part was once a drawing of a bronze vessel (用) used for offerings that would channel intuitive insights. Together, the two parts of the first character describe individuals united by a common source. The lower character is a repeat of the pictogram for humans (人), suggesting awareness or* mind.

THE WAY OF SUBTLE INFLUENCE

Superior leaders are those whose existence is merely known;
     The next best are loved and honored;
The next are respected;
     And the next are ridiculed.

Those who lack belief
Will not in turn be believed.
But when the command comes from afar
And the work is done, the goal achieved,
The people say, "We did it naturally."

Subtle authority is particularly suited to the psychology of those who would be led.
When leaders become overbearing and interfere with the lives of their subjects, the
task of leading becomes unnatural. But when leaders hold back and establish goals
indirectly — through trusting and carefully worded commands — the people find
satisfaction in their work and become more productive. By not interfering, Evolved
Leaders are able to remain unobtrusive. As a result, they gain power from the
people's sense of self-government. The more they conceal their power, the more
effectively it can be used. Evolved Leaders are impartial, intuitive, and aware. Their
influence and power come because they put their energy into guiding rather than
ruling.

The word *naturally* (*tzu jan*) can be literally translated as "self-so."
It refers to an event that occurs as a matter of course. In modern
usage, *tzu jan* also refers to the study of the natural sciences.

悠兮其貴言。功成事遂。百姓皆謂我自然

信不足焉。有不信焉。

太上下知有之。其次親而譽之。其次畏之。其次侮之

HARMONY

The character for harmony (和) *is composed of two parts. The first part* (禾) *was originally the symbol for a grain plant* (米). *The second part symbolizes a mouth* (口). *Together, they imply that grain agrees pleasantly with the mouth and the body, producing a natural harmony.*

LOSING THE INSTINCTS

When the great Tao is forgotten,
    Philanthropy and morality appear.
Intelligent strategies are produced,
    And great hypocrisies emerge.

When the Family has no Harmony,
    Piety and devotion appear.
The nation is confused by chaos,
    And loyal patriots emerge.

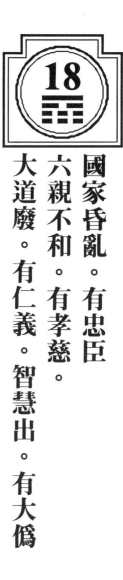

Those who follow the Tao believe that human instincts are inherently compassionate and good. When individuals lose touch with their inner nature and the Tao, however, righteousness and loyalty are created by the intellect to remedy the ensuing social deterioration. Therefore only when a society is corrupt does morality become an issue. Only when personal relationships have become false-hearted do people speak of piety and devotion. And, only when a nation is divided does the patriotic spirit arise. According to Lao Tzu, the enforcement of the "virtues" described in this passage do violence to the human instincts: they deaden spontaneity and rob people of their emotional independence and their sense of personal power. Those who preach morality have lost the Way; those who rely on external systems to interpret their experiences are also adrift.

The word *Family* can be literally translated as "the six relationships." These relationships are parent-child, older sibling-younger sibling, and husband-wife; and they refer, metaphorically, to all social relationships.

The word *philanthropy* comes from the Chinese *jen.* It is sometimes translated as "humanity," "benevolence," or "goodness," yet none of these accurately express the practice of *jen. Jen* refers to social conduct that brings progress and order to society. Although the concept is a benevolent one, Lao Tzu felt it could too easily develop motive and lose its value.

PURITY

Purity (素) *is derived from the character for raw, unrefined silk. In its original form (* 素 *) the ideogram depicted several threads (* 巾 *) obtained from the cocoons of silkworms (* 옷 *) found on the branches of the mulberry tree (* 산산 *).*

RETURN TO SIMPLICITY

Discard the sacred, abandon strategies;
    The people will benefit a hundredfold.
Discard philanthropy, abandon morality;
    The people will return to natural love.
Discard cleverness, abandon the acquisitive;
    The thieves will exist no longer.

However, if these three passages are inadequate,
    Adhere to these principles:
        Perceive purity;
        Embrace simplicity;
        Reduce self-interest;
        Limit desires.

Those who follow the Tao do not rely upon social techniques that must be learned. Even philanthropy and morality are externally imposed ways of civilized behavior that emerge in societies where useful instincts are lost and people no longer trust themselves. Evolved Individuals strive to be intuitive, spontaneous, and simple. From this base they travel lighter, journey farther, and survive longer.

    Leaders are instructed in this passage to use attitude as a form of influence in order to transform their subjects. How is this accomplished? Perceive and acknowledge integrity whenever it appears; attach less emphasis to self-interest; and limit desires by learning to recognize that the greatest happiness in life comes in moments of the purest simplicity.

The word *simplicity*, which appears here and throughout the *Tao Te Ching*, comes from the Chinese word *p'u.* It is translated today as "plain" or "simple," but originally it referred to wood before it was carved. It may also be translated as "uncarved block."

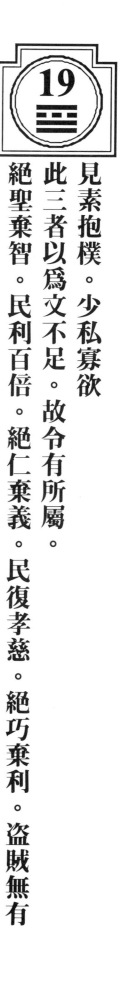

DEVELOPING INDEPENDENCE

Discard the academic; have no anxiety.
How much difference is there between agreement and servility?
How much difference is there between good and evil?
That one should revere what others revere — how absurd and uncentered!

The Collective Mind is expansive and flourishing,
    As if receiving a great sacrifice,
        As if ascending a living observatory.
I alone remain uncommitted,
    Like an infant who has not yet smiled,
        Unattached, without a place to merge.
The Collective Mind is all-encompassing.
    I alone seem to be overlooked.
        I am unknowing to the core and unclear, unclear!

Ordinary people are bright and obvious;
    I alone am dark and obscure.
Ordinary people are exacting and sharp;
    I alone am subdued and dull.

Indifferent like the sea,
    Ceaseless like a penetrating wind,
        The Collective Mind is ever present.
And yet, I alone am unruly and remote.
    I alone am different from the others
        In treasuring nourishment from the Mother.

Using the voice of the accomplished Taoist, Lao Tzu urges those seeking significance in life to step out of the crowd — to discard dogma and explore the universe with intellectual independence. In order to become centered and evolved, one must remain unattached and uncommitted to any ideology. The truth about reality cannot come through words but only through direct experience. Whether seeking the reality in a relationship, in a government, or in a universe, it can only be known with the intuitive mind.

Evolved Individuals not only contribute to the collective awareness of humankind, but they use their global perspective (the living observatory) to know the Tao (the Mother) and ascertain the direction of evolution. They are never obvious or exacting because they realize that such extremes only lead to the collapse of systems and individuals; and they never fall completely into step with the current society because they also hear the voice of the future.

The term *Collective Mind* can also be translated as "collective humanity," "all people," or "the multitude." Here it is interpreted to mean the collective unconscious — a continuous source of information that comes "without learning."

絕學無憂。唯之與阿相去幾何？善之與惡相去何若？

不可不畏人之所畏荒兮其未央哉　眾人熙熙。如享太牢。

如登春臺。我獨泊兮其未兆。如嬰兒之未孩。儽儽兮若無所歸。

眾人皆有餘。而我獨若遺。我愚人之心也哉沌沌兮　俗人昭昭。

我獨昏昏。俗人察察。我獨悶悶　澹兮其若海。飂兮若無止。

眾人皆有以。而我獨頑似鄙。我獨異於人。而貴食於母

LIFE FORCE

In the character life force (精) *the symbols for purity and growth are combined to suggest vigor and refinement. The first symbol (米) shows rice grains (火) that have been thrashed and separated (十), thus purified. It is combined with the symbol for life, the color green (青), which is composed of two parts. The first is the pictogram for a living plant (生) sprouting from the earth, and the other is the alchemist's stove (冎) used to refine and distill matter to its essence.*

KNOWING THE COLLECTIVE ORIGIN

The natural expression of Power
    Proceeds only through the Tao.
The Tao acts through Natural Law;
    So formless, so intangible.

Intangible, formless!
    At its center appears the Image.
Formless, intangible!
    At its center appears Natural Law.
Obscure, mysterious!
    At its center appears the Life Force.
The Life Force is very real;
    At its center appears truth.

From ancient times to the present,
Its name ever remains,
Through the experience of the Collective Origin.

How do I know the way of the Collective Origin?
Through this.

Like the force of a powerful magnet, the Tao cannot be perceived through the senses and is in evidence only through its effect on the myriad things in the universe. The Tao is an informed force. It brings Power to individuals who are aware of it because the collective-unconscious urges and social trends of a culture parallel exactly the physical laws that operate through the Tao. Philosophically, this is one of the most important passages in the *Tao Te Ching*. It suggests that the origins of the Tao can be sensed through an intuitive experience, a thought experiment, of the very beginnings of all reality (the Collective Origin). Evolved Individuals contemplate the interdependent cohesiveness of all matter and energy — a state similar to the one that preceded the Big Bang. Then they reach farther back and identify with the Absolute — a creative state that exists outside of time and space, ever engaged in originating realities such as this one.

The term *Life Force* (*ching*) can also be translated as "essence" or "spirit." In modern Chinese usage, it is also the word for semen.

孔德之容。惟道是從。道之爲物。惟恍惟惚。惚兮恍兮。其中有象。

恍兮惚兮。其中有物。窈兮冥兮。其中有精。其精甚眞。其中有信

自古及今。其名不去。以閱衆甫　吾何以知衆甫之狀哉？以此

FOLLOWING THE PATTERN

What is curved becomes whole;
    What is crooked becomes straight.
What is deep becomes filled;
    What is exhausted becomes refreshed.
What is small becomes attainable;
    What is excessive becomes confused.

Thus Evolved Individuals hold to the One
And regard the world as their Pattern.

They do not display themselves;
    Therefore they are illuminated.
They do not define themselves;
    Therefore they are distinguished.
They do not make claims;
    Therefore they are credited.
They do not boast;
    Therefore they advance.

Since, indeed, they do not compete,
The world cannot compete with them.

That ancient saying: "What is curved becomes whole"—
    Are these empty words?
To become whole,
    Turn within.

Lao Tzu realized that many of the physical laws in nature are reflected in the affairs of society. He saw a pattern of change that was independent of the movements of the solar system; not governed by the passage of time, but instead governed by cause and effect. The Taoist goal is to control cause and effect by transcending it through balance and harmony with the environment. Evolved Individuals regard an obvious and aggressive attempt to gain power and position as a dangerous cause that may result in an uncontrolled effect. They achieve their aims by consolidating their personal power — drawing within the energy that comes from universal awareness and personal accomplishment — rather than spending it on external appearances. Thus they develop intellectual gravity — a powerful social force. In social situations and throughout the physical universe, events are inextricably linked to the distribution of gravity among the participants.

22

曲則全。枉則直。窪則盈。敝則新。少則得。多則惑

是以聖人抱一。爲天下式

不自見。故明。不自是。故彰。

不自伐。故有功。不自矜。故長

夫唯不爭。故天下莫能與之爭

古之所謂曲則全者。豈虛言哉？誠全而。歸之

THE STEADY FORCE OF ATTITUDE

Nature rarely speaks.
    Hence the whirlwind does not last a whole morning,
    Nor the sudden rainstorm last a whole day.
What causes these?
Heaven and Earth.
If Heaven and Earth cannot make them long lasting,
How much less so can humans?

Thus, those who cultivate the Tao
    Identify with the Tao.
Those who cultivate Power
    Identify with Power.
Those who cultivate failure
    Identify with failure.

Those who identify with the Tao
    Are likewise welcomed by the Tao.
Those who identify with Power
    Are likewise welcomed by Power.
Those who identify with failure
    Are likewise welcomed by failure.

Those who lack belief
Will not in turn be believed.

Aggressive movements toward one's aims, like whirlwinds and downpours, have no lasting effect. Violent actions cannot be sustained, and they ultimately generate reactions that neutralize their force. Thus nature rarely speaks, and when it does, it expresses the exception that proves the rule: The principal force in nature is one of steady, harmonious transformation. Those who follow the Tao know that heated confrontations do not yield long-term results. Only attitudes that can be sustained will have the power to alter reality.

The Power discussed in this passage and throughout the *Tao Te Ching* is power over one's continuing reality. Personal power brings independence and freedom into the life of the individual, and it is continuously cultivated through attitude and projection. What one believes, one becomes. The more of a "mind" one has to believe with, the more profound the transformation. Power over others, conversely, is an insidious form of enslavement.

23

希言自然。故飄風不終朝。

驟雨不終日。孰爲此者？而況於人乎？

天地。天地尚不能久。同於道。德者。同於德。失者。同於失

故從事於道者。道亦樂得之。同於德者。德亦樂得之。

同於道者。道亦樂得之。同於德者。德亦樂得之。

同於失者。失亦樂得之　信不足焉。有不信焉

NATURAL LAW

The character for natural law *(物) is the term for matter, and it consists of a sketch of an ox seen from behind (半), with its head, horns, two legs, and tail. It is combined with a character that functions solely as a phonetic modifier (勿). In ancient times, the ox was the most valuable of possessions because its existence strengthened the survival of its possessor.*

THE DANGER IN EXCESS

Those who are on tiptoe cannot stand firm.
Those who straddle cannot walk.
Those who display themselves cannot illuminate.
Those who define themselves cannot be distinguished.
Those who make claims can have no credit.
Those who boast cannot advance.

To those who stay with the Tao,
These are like excess food and redundant actions
And are contrary to Natural Law.
Thus those who possess the Tao turn away.

Individuals who attempt to gain visibility (on tiptoe), who are hypocritical (who straddle), or who boast of achievements, will be overwhelmed by negative counter-reactions. This comes about through a natural group psychology that seeks to balance itself against individuals who attempt to manipulate events. Evolved Individuals recognize the danger of self-serving, self-indulgent conduct within a group. They regard excess and redundancy as the signs of an unbalanced, unstable situation. Because they understand the physical laws in nature, they realize that the outcome of any excess is rapid decline. Therefore, they quietly remove themselves. They discard social fixations because they have discovered the richness of simplicity.

其在道也。曰餘食贅行。物或惡之。故有道者不處

自伐者無功。自矜者不長

企者不立。跨者不行。自見者不明。自是者不彰。

THE TAO OF GREATNESS

There was something in a state of fusion
Before Heaven and Earth were born.

Silent, vast,
     Independent, and unchanging;
Working everywhere, tirelessly;
     It can be regarded as Mother of the world.
I do not know its name;
     The word I say is Tao.
Forced to give it a name,
     I say Great.

Great means continuing.
Continuing means going far.
Going far means returning.

Therefore the Tao is Great.
Heaven and Earth are Great.
A leader is likewise Great.
In the universe there are four Greatnesses,
And leadership is one of them.

Humans are modeled on the earth.
     The earth is modeled on heaven.
Heaven is modeled on the Tao.
     The Tao is modeled on nature.

The first two lines in this passage describe the Taoist view of the period shortly after the beginning of the universe when the Tao came into existence but all matter and energy remained one cohesive and undifferentiated substance. Theoretical physicists, searching for a single interaction, or unified field, at the heart of the universe, might describe this state as one that existed seconds before the Big Bang. In the first billionth of a second after the beginning of the Big Bang, the four forces appeared (gravity, strong nuclear force, electromagnetism, and weak nuclear force), and energy and matter, time and space, were differentiated. Lao Tzu calls the actions of the physical forces throughout the universe and in the social patterns of human beings, the Tao.

The term *Great* in this passage refers to the Tao and its cyclic movements through reality. Because it goes far, it returns — or, given enough time, history repeats itself. The movements of the Tao follow the laws of the physical forces, and the Power (*Te*) of Taoism lies in perceiving and understanding the manifestations of those laws in society. Evolved Leaders intuitively perceive the Tao in the evolution of society, and thus they are able to guide those whom they lead to harmony and fulfillment.

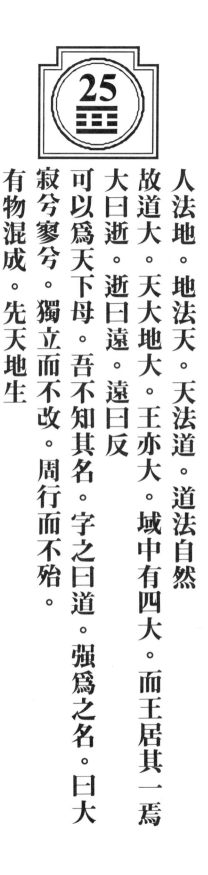

有物混成。先天地生

寂兮寥兮。獨立而不改。周行而不殆。

可以為天下母。吾不知其名。字之曰道。強為之名。曰大

大曰逝。逝曰遠。遠曰反

故道大。天大地大。王亦大。域中有四大。而王居其一焉

人法地。地法天。天法道。道法自然

THE EMPEROR CH'IEN LUNG

*Ch'ien Lung (A.D. 1710-1799), the grandson of the brilliant Emperor K'ang Hsi,
was the classic model of the educated, cultivated ruler. As a child he showed such
remarkable gifts of intellect and talent that his grandfather decided this precocious
boy would one day have the throne. He was thoroughly educated in the arts,
literature, horsemanship, archery, and the skills of military strategy and tactics.
In 1735, at the age of twenty-four, Ch'ien Lung was proclaimed emperor.*

*During the first ten years, his reign became a succession of internal wars, which
eventually calmed. For the next fifty years the empire enjoyed peace and prosperity
while the population nearly doubled to 200 million. Ch'ien Lung concentrated on
China's cultural development. He ordered a search for all literary works worthy of
preservation and commissioned a descriptive catalogue of the Imperial Library,
which included not only the history of each work, but also a detailed
academic critique of it. After sixty successful years of power, Ch'ien Lung
abdicated in favor of his son.*

The Metropolitan Museum of Art, New York

THE GRAVITY OF POWER

Gravity is the foundation of levity.
Stillness is the master of agitation.

Thus Evolved Individuals can travel the whole day
    Without leaving behind their baggage.
However arresting the views,
    They remain calm and unattached.
How can leaders with ten thousand chariots
    Have a light-hearted position in the world?

If they are light-hearted, they lose their foundation.
If they are agitated, they lose their mastery.

It is the responsibility of Evolved Leaders to create a calm center that will serve as the foundation for their organizations. Regardless of the stimulating diversions in their path, they must retain their composure and sense of purpose. They do not let themselves become separated from their "baggage," and thus they maintain their position through serious-mindedness. The concept of "ten thousand chariots" was an unimaginably formidable power to the ancient Chinese, perhaps something on the scale of nuclear power today. Lao Tzu believed that leaders with such power have an awesome responsibility and can be neither light-hearted nor agitated.

The term *baggage* can also be translated as "loaded cart" or "baggage wagon," and has the metaphorical meaning of gravity or seriousness.

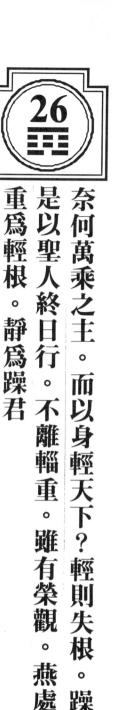

THE SKILLFUL EXCHANGE OF INFORMATION

A good path has no ruts.
A good speech has no flaws.
A good analysis uses no schemes.

A good lock has no bar or bolt,
　　And yet it cannot be opened.
A good knot does not restrain,
　　And yet it cannot be unfastened.

Thus Evolved Individuals are always good at saving others;
　　Hence no one is wasted.
They are always good at saving things;
　　Hence nothing is wasted.

This is called Doubling the Light.

Therefore a good person is the teacher of an inferior person;
　　And an inferior person is the resource of a good person.
One who does not treasure a teacher, or does not cherish a resource,
　　Although intelligent, is greatly deluded.

This is called Significant Subtlety.

When individuals use force and manipulative methods to shape events, they are walking a path that is already rutted, using logic that is inherently flawed, and basing their calculations on schemes and guesses. Just as the most skillful knots and locks can hold things in place without excessive force, certain ends are best accomplished without the use of obvious means. In worldly undertakings, the most effective and far-reaching systems rely upon spontaneity, creativity, and an intuitive understanding of human nature and social needs.

Evolved Individuals skillfully employ people and things, and thus spread the Light: the information that helps steer the course of evolution. In this way, the skillful person becomes a teacher. Herein lies the symbiotic relationship that reflects the interdependence between all states in the universe: energy and matter, proton and electron, time and space. Inferior (or uninformed) individuals require for their fulfillment and growth a model after which they can pattern themselves. Teachers derive energy and penetrating insight from acting as that model. Thus, with the proper values and attitudes toward each other, they are both transformed and come into harmony and accord with the Tao.

The word *schemes*, sometimes translated as "counting chips" or "tallies," is actually derived from the name of a bamboo device used in divination. In modern usage, this phrase might be translated as "plans or stratagems."

善行無轍跡。善言無瑕讁。善數不用籌策

善閉無關楗。而不可開。善結無繩約。而不可解

是以聖人。常善救人。

故無棄人。常善救物。故無棄物　是謂襲明

故善人者不善人之師。不善人者善人之資。

不貴其師不愛其資。雖智大迷　是謂要妙

27

UNITING THE FORCES

Know the male,
    Hold to the female;
        Become the world's stream.
By being the world's stream,
    The Power will never leave.
        This is returning to Infancy.

Know the white,
    Hold to the black;
        Become the world's pattern.
By becoming the world's pattern,
    The Power will never falter.
        This is returning to Limitlessness.

Know the glory,
    Hold to the obscurity;
        Become the world's valley.
By being the world's valley,
    The Power will be sufficient.
        This is returning to Simplicity.

When Simplicity is broken up,
It is made into instruments.
Evolved Individuals who employ them,
Are made into leaders.
In this way the Great System is united.

Unwavering Power is bestowed on Evolved Individuals who are able to direct the talents of otherwise unconnected individuals into a collective endeavor. Just as reservoirs collect water, leaders become low spots for the exchange of power and information. They are aware of the instability in aggression and obviousness. To hold their position they are receptive, subtle, and modest.

In physics, the four forces in the universe are those forces engaged in holding matter together (gravity, strong nuclear force, weak nuclear force, and electromagnetism). In the Taoist view, leaders who imitate those forces by connecting individuals and evolving society are given the Power to alter reality. In this passage, Lao Tzu uses the images of Infancy, Limitlessness, and Simplicity to describe the intuitive understanding of the Great System: the united field of matter and energy as it existed prior to the beginnings of the known universe. To know this is to perceive the Tao.

知其雄。守其雌。爲天下谿。爲天下谿。常德不離。復歸於嬰兒

知其白。守其黑。爲天下式。爲天下式。常德不忒。復歸於無極

知其榮。守其辱。爲天下谷。

爲天下谷。常德乃足。復歸於樸

樸散。則爲器。聖人用之。

則爲官長。故大制不割

EMPEROR YAO

The Emperor Yao (died 2258 B.C.) is one of China's great legendary emperors. He ascended the throne in 2357 B.C. and toured his domain from time to time to inspect its condition. His reign is known as one of contentment and social stability. At his retirement, he chose to bypass his worthless son Tan Chu and abdicate his throne in favor of a gifted farmer named Shun, thereby setting the precedent of handing down the throne to the worthy and deserving.

Emperor Yao understood clearly the importance of leadership and believed that strong social order was based on universal patterns, which he did his best to record. He kept a record of astronomical observations — the cycles of the moon and planetary revolutions — and compiled a calendar consisting of 360 days and four seasons. Thus he is credited with teaching his people to regulate agriculture by sowing seeds at the proper seasons.

The National Palace Museum, Taipei, Taiwan

THE WAY OF NONINTERFERENCE

Those who would take hold of the world and act on it,
Never, I notice, succeed.

The world is a mysterious instrument,
    Not made to be handled.
Those who act on it, spoil it.
    Those who seize it, lose it.

So, in Natural Law
    Some lead, some follow;
    Some agitate, some remain silent;
    Some are firm, some are weak;
    Some carry on, some lose heart.

Thus, Evolved Individuals
    Avoid extremes,
    Avoid extravagance,
    Avoid excess.

All systems have hidden within them a natural geometry. Crystals form and cells replicate within a strict mathematical organization. Thus, to interfere with the natural state of people or events is a futile and often tragic endeavor. In social systems, Evolved Individuals observe and understand this natural state and then position themselves appropriately. They are always in harmony with the deeper trends in the evolution of society. They exert the force of their convictions through a state of focused inner awareness, while externally they practice strategic noninterference. Those who follow the Tao are reluctant to push things to the extreme, even to extremes of complacency, for they know that this can lead to undesirable counter-reactions. Instead they strive to maintain their intellectual balance by experiencing the rhythms of natural events with emotional independence.

將欲取天下而為之。吾見其不得已　天下神器。不可為也。

為者敗之。執者失之。故物。或行或隨。或歔或吹。

或强或贏。或載或隳　是以聖人。去甚。去奢。去泰

LEADING THE LEADER

Those who use the Tao to guide leaders
Do not use forceful strategies in the world.
Such matters tend to recoil.

Where armies are positioned,
Thorny brambles are produced.
A great military always brings years of hunger.

Those who are skillful
Succeed and then stop.
They dare not hold on with force.

They succeed and do not boast.
They succeed and do not make claims.
They succeed and are not proud.
They succeed and do not acquire in excess.
They succeed and do not force.

Things overgrown will always decline.
This is not the Tao.
What is not the Tao will soon end.

Organizations that confuse offense with defense and aggression with protection invariably deplete their resources and lead their people into times of hunger. Organizations have great momentum and do not know how to stop their forward motion. Therefore those who advise leaders are responsible for holding the organization back from the excess that leads to collapse. Those who design forceful strategies to use against other organizations are not fit to advise leaders, because the nature of their work — as necessary as it may be — limits their intellectual capacity to apprehend the evolution of society (the Tao). Evolved Individuals know that it is possible to achieve success without planting the seeds of self-destruction. Therefore they are not aggressive and they are not acquisitive. Only individuals with such characteristics are fit to guide the leader of an organization.

30

以道佐人主者。不以兵強天下。其事好還

師之所處。荊棘生焉。大軍之後必有凶年

善者。果而已。不敢以取強

果而勿矜。果而勿伐。果而勿驕。

果而不得已。果而勿強

物壯則老。是謂不道。不道早已

THE USE OF FORCE

The finest weapons can be the instruments of misfortune,
And thus contrary to Natural Law.
Those who possess the Tao turn away from them.
Evolved leaders occupy and honor the left;
Those who use weapons honor the right.

Weapons are instruments of misfortune
    That are used by the unevolved.
When their use is unavoidable,
    The superior act with calm restraint.

Even when victorious, let there be no joy,
    For such joy leads to contentment with slaughter.
Those who are content with slaughter
    Cannot find fulfillment in the world.

The use of force to alter worldly events is regarded in this passage as a sometimes necessary evil. The "finest weapon" might be a powerful army or may be as subtle as a sharp intellect or a clever strategy — yet when it is used to exert force over another, it is "contrary to Natural Law." Thus there will be an unfortunate counter-reaction.

When the use of force is unavoidable, Evolved leaders practice restraint. Furthermore, they know that force will enhance personal power only to the extent that it is regrettable. Once victory is achieved, they do not allow themselves to feel joy; instead, they express regret. Their attitude strongly affects their organization, and thus internal conflicts are regarded as a matter of sorrow as well. Therefore a regretful attitude in leaders during times of external force can have a calming and peaceful effect on the internal affairs of the organization.

The word *left* refers to the left hand — the hand most reluctant to reach out and act. The right hand is associated with strength and assertiveness. This idea was further elaborated upon by Wang Pi (c. 226-249), who wrote one of the earliest commentaries on the *Tao Te Ching*, in a passage often attached to Lao Tzu's:

On the left, undertakings bring good fortune.
    On the right, undertakings bring misfortune.
The second in command occupies the left;
    The commander occupies the right.
That is, they arrange themselves as in rites of mourning.

For the slaughter of many,
    Let us grieve with heartfelt sorrow.
For a victory in battle,
    Let us receive it with rites of mourning.

31

夫佳兵者不祥之器。物或惡之。故有道者不處。
君子居則貴左。用兵則貴右
兵者不祥之器。非君子之器。不得已而用之。恬淡爲上
勝而不美。而美之者是樂殺人。
夫樂殺人者。
則不可得志於天下矣

SIMPLICITY

The first part of the character for simplicity *(樸) is the symbol for tree (木), with its trunk (｜), branches (一), and roots (八). This is combined with the ideogram for gathering wood into a bundle (業), which in its ancient form (叢) was made up of hands (𠂇彐) collecting twigs and branches (半).*

THE LIMITS OF SPECIALIZATION

The Tao of the Absolute has no name.
Although infinitesimal in its Simplicity,
The world cannot master it.

If leaders would hold on to it,
    All Things would naturally follow.
Heaven and Earth would unite to rain Sweet Dew,
    And people would naturally cooperate without commands.

Names emerge when institutions begin.
When names emerge, know likewise to stop.
To know when to stop is to be free of danger.

The presence of the Tao in the world
Is like the valley stream joining the rivers and seas.

In this passage, Lao Tzu advises leaders to move toward simplicity and away from complexity — toward universality rather than differentiation. As always, he urges leaders to learn when to stop and practice noninterference. Leaders who insist on exacting systems and roles in their organizations cannot create a natural, effortless atmosphere for the completion of tasks, because the structure they conceive of is suited for machines, not humans. When people are forced into roles and every aspect of their work defined, their possibilities become limited, they no longer create, and they do not evolve. When leaders systematize every detail in their organization, they close it off from the possibility of evolution. Just as life forms that are highly specialized move in the direction of extinction, this path leads to the extinction of the organization. On the other hand, with open-ended management the people have nothing to resist or resent. They become spontaneously cooperative because their attention shifts to the end rather than the means.

The term *Sweet Dew* comes from the Chinese myth that when a kingdom is at complete peace, the morning dew tastes like honey.

道常無名。樸雖小。天下莫能臣也　侯王若能守之。萬物將自賓。

天地相合以降甘露。民莫之令而自均　始制有名。名亦既有夫亦將知止。

知止可以不殆　譬道之在天下。猶川谷之於江海

INSIGHT

To have insight (明) is to have the radiance of the sun (⊙), a symbol that later took a modern form (日), and the clarity of the moon (月), which was originally symbolized with a crescent (☽).

SELF-MASTERY

Those who know others are intelligent;
    Those who know themselves have insight.
Those who master others have force;
    Those who master themselves have strength.

Those who know what is enough are wealthy.
    Those who persevere have direction.
Those who maintain their position endure.
    And those who die and yet do not perish, live on.

Self-knowledge and self-mastery are the primary Taoist accomplishments. They are achieved when individuals cultivate the inner mind, refining their instincts and intuitive responses to the world. The result is insight: the ability to perceive the larger influences behind specific social phenomena. To know the inner mind and perceive its connection with the evolving mind of the universe is the foundation for foresight and lasting influence. Through inner knowledge, one develops the ability to alter the world through small, effortless actions at the very beginning of events. It is essential to discriminate between clever force and insightful strength, for only the latter will not meet with resistance or cause counter-reactions. Those who "die and yet do not perish," are those who leave the affairs of the world in a more evolved state than they found them.

不失其所者久。死而不亡者壽

知足者富。強行者有志。

知人者智。自知者明。勝人者有力。自勝者強

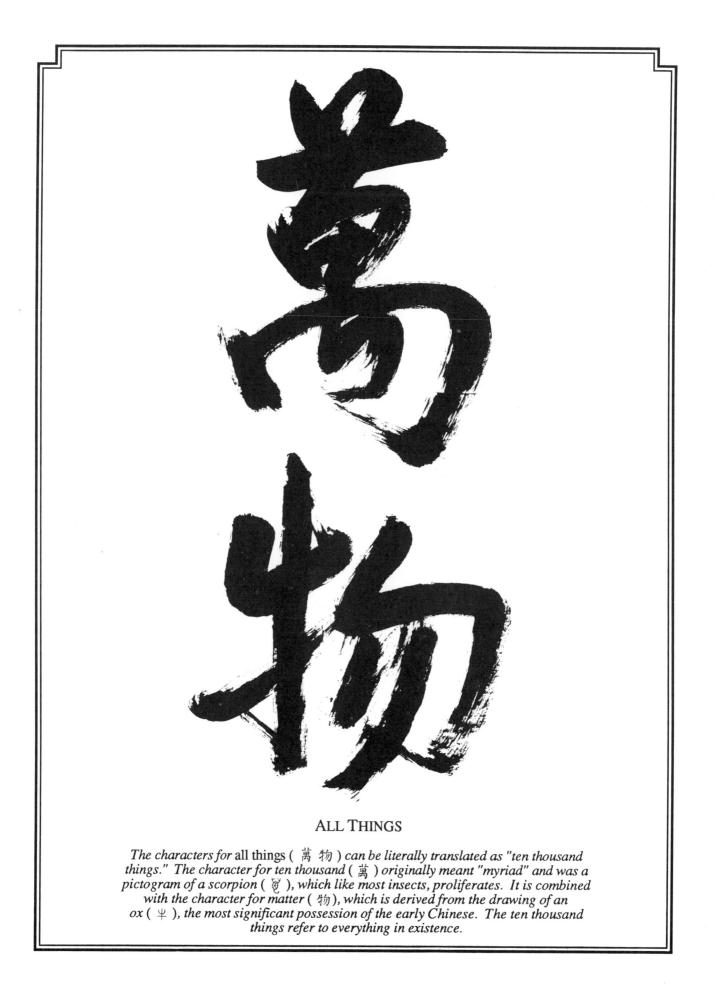

ALL THINGS

The characters for all things (萬 物) *can be literally translated as "ten thousand things." The character for ten thousand (萬) originally meant "myriad" and was a pictogram of a scorpion (𧌒), which like most insects, proliferates. It is combined with the character for matter (物), which is derived from the drawing of an ox (半), the most significant possession of the early Chinese. The ten thousand things refer to everything in existence.*

THE EVOLVING TAO

The Great Tao extends everywhere.
It is on the left and the right.

All Things depend on it for growth,
And it does not deny them.
It achieves its purpose,
And it does not have a name.
It clothes and cultivates All Things,
And it does not act as master.

Always without desire,
It can be named Small.
All Things merge with it,
And it does not act as master.
It can be named Great.

In the end it does not seek greatness,
And in that way the Great is achieved.

The Tao, as described in this passage, is a force that is evolving all matter and energy. It does so spontaneously and naturally, without motive or possessiveness. Those who follow the Tao evolve their social environments in the same way. They instinctively and deftly untangle the knots and smooth the fabric of life and allow the needs for growth, creativity, and independence in those around them to be fulfilled. People are drawn to inspiring individuals who allow greatness (the Tao) to work through them. Lao Tzu believed that to emulate the behavior of the Tao would bring individuals into the closest possible harmony with actual reality and true meaning in life. A life that shares, in its aims, the purpose of the universe, will also share in its greatness and significance.

大道汜兮。其可左右　萬物恃之而生。而不辭。功成。不名有。

衣養萬物。而不爲主　常無欲。可名於小。萬物歸焉。而不爲主。

可名爲大　以其終不自爲大。故能成其大

GREAT IMAGE

The concept of great (大) *is symbolized by a human form with the arms stretched out to their limit. This character is combined with the ideogram for* image (象), *a modification of a primitive drawing of an elephant (豫) showing the trunk (⌒), tusks (⌣), and body with legs and tail (豸). An elephant is the symbol for image due, in part, to its large size and memorable shape.*

SENSING THE INSENSIBLE

Hold fast to the Great Image,
    And all the world will come.
Yet its coming brings no harm,
    Only peace and order.

When there is music together with food,
    The audience will linger.
But when the Tao is expressed,
    It seems without substance or flavor.

We observe and there is nothing to see.
We listen and there is nothing to hear.
We use it and it is without end.

This passage describes a state of mind — a thought experiment — leading to an awareness of the interconnectedness and interdependence of all things. Lao Tzu cautions that the contemplation of the Tao may seem dull or difficult since it is not apprehensible through the senses. Yet, he promises that an awareness of the cohesiveness in the universe — the Great Image — will bring to the beholder a rich and powerful understanding. The key to the Taoist perspective is to experience this sense of cohesiveness and complete integration with one's environment while functioning effectively in the outside world. Such lives take on extraordinary meaning.

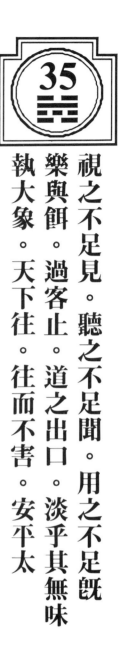

執大象。天下往。往而不害。安平太
樂與餌。過客止。道之出口。淡乎其無味
視之不足見。聽之不足聞。用之不足既

EMPEROR T'AI TSU OF THE SUNG DYNASTY

*Chao K'uang-yin, known as the Emperor T'ai Tsu, founded the Sung Dynasty and
ruled China from A.D. 960 to 976. Descended from a long line of officials, T'ai Tsu
rose to high military command. Because of his reputation for using authority fairly,
his men looked to him for guidance during the disturbed state of the new empire.
To reunify the war-torn nation, he placed the military under strong control and used
diplomatic processes instead. He selected his officials from the ranks of the learned,
and impressed on his military officers the need for study.*

*T'ai Tsu made his magistrates directly responsible to him, and during battle
he commanded that there be no wholesale slaughter or looting of property. Emperor
T'ai Tsu was frugal by nature and he forbade excessive luxury in his government,
declaring that the empire was a great trust that he held. As a result, the
contemplation of nature's beauty became the major theme in the art throughout
the Sung Dynasty. After fifteen years of beneficial rule, he abdicated in
favor of his brother, T'ai Tsung.*

The National Palace Museum, Taipei, Taiwan

CONCEALING THE ADVANTAGE

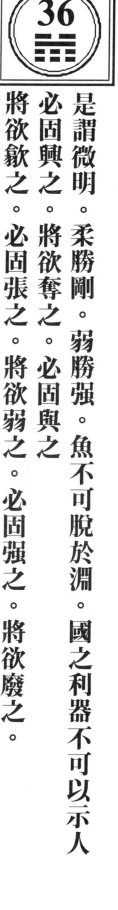

In order to deplete it,
    It must be thoroughly extended.
In order to weaken it,
    It must be thoroughly strengthened.
In order to reject it,
    It must be thoroughly promoted.
In order to take away from it,
    It must be thoroughly endowed.

This is called a Subtle Insight.
    The yielding can triumph over the inflexible;
    The weak can triumph over the strong.
Fish should not be taken from deep waters;
Nor should organizations make obvious their advantages.

Organizations with the highest strategic advantage are those with the greatest potential for loss. When an organization becomes overextended, when it complacently accepts praise and promotion, gifts and abundant profits, when it believes itself to be growing ever stronger — it is then that it is most vulnerable. It has become unstable within the natural cycle of polarity and is on a path leading toward its opposite state. Because "fish" taken from the watery depths cannot survive, organizations should keep their advantages out of sight and out of action. Advantages that are restrained are more effective and long-lasting than those that are displayed because concealed advantages do not cause resistance or counter-reactions.

Inherent in this passage are instructions for a smaller organization that would overcome a larger one. The principle behind "Subtle Insight" is one that is frequently repeated in the *Tao Te Ching*: The weak can overcome the strong by yielding and contributing to the excessiveness of the strong. Excessiveness germinates the seed that forces things to grow into their opposite.

LEADER

In its most original form, the character for leader (王) *was a pictogram of three jade beads (⋮) threaded together ( ). Since only a wealthy and powerful individual could afford to possess such stones, the pictogram became synonymous with the word for ruler. More recent descriptions state that the character depicts an upright individual ( ) vested with the power to unite the planes of heaven (¯), earth (＿), and humanity (⁻).*

THE POWER IN DESIRELESSNESS

The Tao never acts,
And yet is never inactive.

If leaders can hold on to it,
    All Things will be naturally influenced.
Influenced and yet desiring to act,
    I would calm them with Nameless Simplicity.
Nameless Simplicity is likewise without desire;
    And without desire there is harmony.

The world will then be naturally stabilized.

Lao Tzu believed that the best leaders were those with the intellectual and emotional strength to guide rather than rule. Evolved Leaders put all of their energies into leading the way, and they do not interfere with the lives of their followers. Thus people are influenced naturally, without resistance, resentment, or reaction. When people do not follow, it is because the leader is moving against the grain of human nature and against the direction of social evolution. Such leaders bring chaos to the world.

    Leaders who hold to the Tao when guiding others are ever active in their own internal growth. In order to align themselves with the trends in society and the movements in nature (the Tao), they practice simplicity in their lives and work. In this way, they avoid the distorted intellectual and emotional growth that comes with any fixation on material possessions or self-aggrandizing social systems. Because they free themselves from irrelevant and misleading desires, they receive insights that bring harmony and stability to everything they touch.

37

道常無爲。而無不爲　侯王若能守之。萬物將自化。

化而欲作。吾將鎭之以無名之樸。

無名之樸夫亦將無欲。不欲以靜　天下將自定

POWER WITHOUT MOTIVE

Superior Power is never Powerful, thus it has Power.
     Inferior Power is always Powerful, thus it has no Power.
Superior Power takes no action and acts without motive.
     Inferior Power takes action and acts with motive.

Superior philanthropy takes action and acts without motive.
     Superior morality takes action and acts with motive.
Superior propriety takes action and there is no response;
     So it raises its arm to project itself.

Therefore, lose the Tao and Power follows.
Lose the Power and philanthropy follows.
Lose philanthropy and morality follows.
Lose morality and propriety follows.

One who has propriety has the veneer of truth
     And yet is the leader of confusion.
One who knows the future has the luster of the Tao
     And yet is ignorant of its origins.

Therefore those with the greatest endurance
     Can enter the substantial,
     Not occupy its veneer;
     Can enter reality,
     Not occupy its luster.
Hence they discard one and receive the other.

Evolved Power is irresistible because it is based on substance and reality and is free of motive. Power that has degenerated into force involves complex strategies and social manipulations because it is based on appearance and illusion. Lao Tzu believed that morality was an invention of leaders who could not find truth in themselves and thus were unable to trust others to conduct themselves appropriately. But even more dangerous to the independent-minded Lao Tzu was propriety — conduct that requires study, memory, and occasional hypocrisy to follow. He believed that propriety would contaminate with motive the inherently good and truthful instincts of humans.

The word *propriety* (*li*) refers to the ceremonies, rituals, and social forms of a culture. *Li* expresses the current standards of social behavior.

38

上德不德是以有德。下德不失德是以無德。上德無爲而無以爲。
下德爲之而有以爲。上仁爲之而無以爲。
上義爲之而有以爲。上禮爲之而莫之應。則攘臂而扔之
故失道而後德。失德而後仁。失仁而後義。失義而後禮
夫禮者忠信之薄。而亂之首。前識者道之華。而愚之始
是以大丈夫。處其厚。不居其薄。處其實。不居其華。故去彼取此

ONENESS IN LEADERSHIP

From old, these may have harmony with the One:

Heaven in harmony with the One becomes clear.
Earth in harmony with the One becomes stable.
Mind in harmony with the One becomes inspired.
Valleys in harmony with the One become full.
All Things in harmony with the One become creative.
Leaders in harmony with the One become incorruptible in the world.

These were attained through Oneness.

Heaven without clarity would probably crack.
Earth without stability would probably quake.
Mind without inspiration would probably sleep.
Valleys without fullness would probably dry up.
All Things without creativity would probably die off.
Leaders without incorruptible ways would probably stumble and fall.

Indeed, the high-placed stem from the humble;
    The elevated are based upon the lowly.
This is why leaders call themselves
    Alone, lonely, and unfavored.
Is this not because they stem from the humble and common?
    Is it not?

Therefore, attain honor without being honored.
Do not desire to shine like jade; wear ornaments as if they were stone.

The state of Oneness described in this passage is the state where there is a cohesive harmony between the one and the many. This is a principal Taoist thought exercise: the ability to sense the interdependence and rhythmic interactions between all matter and energy in the universe. Whether that matter and energy are coalesced into a solar system or a family, into spawning salmon or decaying plutonium — if they are existing simultaneously, they are interdependent. It is in the connections between universal phenomena that the truth of existence can be known.

On the plateau of leadership, this passage implies that leaders must create in themselves a sense of identification with their subjects, who in turn must sense this. Evolved Leaders realize that their position rests on the foundation of those below them. They preserve their position and remain connected to those below through simplicity. They do not desire the trappings of honor and prestige because such things can only separate and block their sense of Oneness with the people. Evolved Leaders are incorruptible because they are in complete identification with those whom they serve and believe the needs of the people to be their own.

39

昔之得一者　天得一以清。地得一以寧。神得一以靈。谷得一以盈。

萬物得一以生。侯王得一以爲天下貞　其致之　天無以清將恐裂。

地無以寧將恐發。神無以靈將恐歇。谷無以盈將恐竭。

萬物無以生將恐滅。侯王無以貞將恐蹶　故貴以賤爲本。

高以下爲基。是以侯王自謂。孤寡不轂。

此非以賤爲本邪？非乎？故致譽無譽。不欲琭琭如玉珞珞如石

POLARITY

The character for polarity (反) has two parts. The first (厂) is symbolic of motion. The second part is an abbreviated form of the hand (又). Combined, they describe the movement of a hand turning over. This character is also translated as "reverse" or "return."

THE WAY

Polarity is the movement of the Tao.
Receptivity is the way it is used.
The world and All Things were produced from its existence.
Its existence was produced from nonexistence.

According to Lao Tzu, it was from nonexistence — the Absolute — that the Tao was produced. The Tao, in turn, produced the positive and negative states *yin* and *yang*. These charged states coalesced into all of physical reality, their behavioral and structural characteristics based on a unified field of forces. These forces, or physical laws, reflect the actions of the Tao. The Tao acts through polarity, a physical law that governs cause and effect. In social realms this manifests in such cycles as easy and difficult or active and passive. The law of polarity changes and evolves all things by acting upon extremes. Extremes are overcharged and begin moving in their opposite direction. Those who follow the Tao avoid extremes and practice moderation and receptivity. In this way they gain power by moving with the prevailing forces.

The word *polarity* is variously translated as "reverse," "return," or "repeat." It is used in the *Tao Te Ching* to describe a key physical law at work in the universe.

40

有生於無

天下萬物生於有。

反者道之動。弱者道之用。

MASTERING THE PARADOX

When superior leaders hear of the Tao,
    They diligently try to practice it.
When average leaders hear of the Tao,
    They appear both aware and unaware of it.
When inferior leaders hear of the Tao,
    They roar with laughter.

Without sufficient laughter, it could not be the Tao;
Hence the long-established sayings:

The Tao illuminated appears to be obscure;
    The Tao advancing appears to be retreating;
        The Tao leveled appears to be uneven.

Superior Power appears to be low;
    Great clarity appears to be spotted;
        Extensive Power appears to be insufficient;
            Established Power appears to be stolen;
                Substantial Power appears to be spurious.

The greatest space has no corners;
    The greatest talents are slowly mastered;
        The greatest music has the rarest sound;
        The Great Image has no form.

The Tao is hidden and nameless,
Yet it is the Tao that skillfully supports and completes.

Those who follow the Tao continually look beyond the present reality in an attempt to perceive the seeds of change. They have complete faith in physical laws that demonstrate that all of reality is in a process of change and all processes cycle in the direction of their opposite — life to death, positive to negative, energy to matter — and back again. Because they learn to recognize and understand the law of polarity, they gain extraordinary insight into worldly affairs.

Evolved Individuals know that people who are not intuitive can be dangerous to work with since they are guided solely by the current appearance of things that are, in reality, changing. Unintuitive actions and decisions lack dimension, and, what is worse, they may interfere insensitively with the natural process of change and cause dangerous counter-reactions. Evolved Individuals seek out others who have intuition and vision — a form of intelligence that comes from cultivating the instincts, observing the direction of change, and apprehending the evolution of ideas.

41

道隱無名。夫唯道善貸且成

大方無隅。大器晚成。大音希聲。大象無形

上德若谷。大白若辱。廣德若不足。建德若偷。質德若渝

不笑不足以爲道。故建言有之　明道若昧。進道若退。夷道若纇

若存若亡。下士聞道。大笑之

上士聞道。勤而行之。中士聞道。

KNOWING POLARITY

The Tao produced the One.
The One produced the Two.
The Two produced the Three.
The Three produced All Things.

All Things carry Yin and hold to Yang;
Their blended Influence brings Harmony.

People hate to be alone, lonely, and unfavored;
And yet leaders take these names.

Thus in Natural Law
    Some lose and in this way profit.
    Some profit and in this way lose.

What others have taught, I also teach:
    Those who are violent do not die naturally.
    I will make this my chief teaching.

This is the most penetrating and succinct of Lao Tzu's descriptions of the formation of the universe. What he does not touch on, in this passage, is the Absolute that produced the Tao. The Absolute stands outside of space and time — outside of the universes it creates. The Tao produced the One: temporal/spatial reality. The One produced the Two: the opposite charges of positive and negative (*yin* and *yang*). The Two produced the Three: matter, energy, and the physical laws that bind them together. From these three came the existence of All Things in the universe. All Things are interconnected and interdependent, and from this concept comes the behavior of polarity: When something increases, something else decreases. Thus Evolved Leaders who wish to endure do not elevate themselves; and those who would like to live out their days are never violent.

LAO TZU RIDING A BUFFALO

The National Palace Museum, Taipei, Taiwan

42

強梁者不得其死。吾將以為敎父
人之所敎我亦敎之。
故物。或損之而益。或益之而損
人之所惡唯孤寡不轂。而王公以為稱
萬物負陰而抱陽。沖氣以為和
道生一。一生二。二生三。三生萬物

SUBTLETY

The character for subtlety ($玄$) *is literally derived from the motion of putting thread into a dark green or black dye. The original ideogram ($\underline{玄}$) depicted silk thread wound from two cocoons (8). This thread was placed in a vat in the same way that a seedling (﹅) inserts its roots (人) into the earth to undergo a transformation. This character is also translated as "mysterious" or "profound."*

SUBTLE POWERS

The most yielding parts of the world
        Overtake the most rigid parts of the world.
                The insubstantial can penetrate continually.

Therefore I know that without action there is advantage.

This philosophy without words,
        This advantage without action —
                It is rare, in the world, to attain them.

Lao Tzu believed that most difficulties in life are born out of reactions to larger effects, and that problems tend to resolve themselves when they are not met with aggression and invited to remain. Just as large ships are steered with small rudders, Lao Tzu felt that when action was necessary, the most subtle effort would yield the most effective result: a result that would not bring along a new set of problems. In the most personal sense, noninterference is a form of freedom — one that can bring power to individuals who have the courage to practice it.

不言之教。無爲之益。天下希及之
吾是以知無爲之有益
天下之至柔。馳騁天下之至堅。無有入無間

老子

PORTRAIT OF LAO TZU

The National Palace Museum, Taipei, Taiwan

THE POWER IN NEEDING LESS

知足。不辱。知止。不殆　可以長久

是故甚愛。必大費。多藏。必厚亡

名與身孰親？身與貨孰多？得與亡孰病？

Which is dearer,
    Name or life?
Which means more,
    Life or wealth?
Which is worse,
    Gain or loss?

The stronger the attachments,
    The greater the cost.
The more that is hoarded,
    The deeper the loss.

Know what is enough;
    Be without disgrace.
Know when to stop;
    Be without danger.

In this way one lasts for a very long time.

In the Taoist view, individuals who are materially oriented — who identify themselves with their possessions — have no real purpose in the universe other than moving matter from place to place and reproducing life forms that may ultimately have the potential for intellectual evolution. Materially oriented individuals cannot evolve intellectually because their attachment to and hoarding of matter trains the mind to view reality as fixed and unflowing. This view is in harmony with dying, not growth, and thus they cannot connect with the larger meaning behind conciousness.

Those who follow the Tao realize that they are in a more powerful position when they are mobile, unburdened, and independent. For the Taoist, excessive possessions are treated like ballast. They are released to gain greater buoyancy. Just as air rushes in to fill a vacuum, more things will come into and pass through such lives. Most important, the capacity to need less and pass things on brings Evolved Individuals closer to themselves and closer to the continuous unfolding of reality — a perspective of advantage in the world.

HSIEH AN AT EAST MOUNTAIN

Hsieh An (A.D. 320-385) was a member of a very distinguished and politically prominent family, although in the early part of his life he preferred to live in retirement, engaged in scholarly pursuits. It was only when his brother, a military commander, got into difficulties that Hsieh An entered official life and rapidly ascended to a post of importance and power. Nevertheless, his preference for contemplation and cultured leisure earned him the title "Refined Minister."

Under his direction, his brother and his nephew set off to halt a nearing invasion. The result of the conflict was anxiously awaited by all, yet Hsieh An had such composure that he passed the time with wei ch'i, a game requiring great concentration and skill. When a courier arrived from the front to say that the enemy had been routed, he read it calmly and, upon being asked by a guest what the news was, he replied: "Merely that my boys have defeated the rebels," and proceeded to finish his game.

The National Palace Museum, Taipei, Taiwan

USING EMPTINESS

If the greatest achievement is incomplete,
    Then its usefulness is unimpaired.
If the greatest fullness is empty,
    Then its usefulness is inexhaustible.

The greatest directness is flexible.
The greatest skillfulness is awkward.
The greatest eloquence is hesitant.

Agitation triumphs over the cold.
Stillness triumphs over the heated.
Clarity and stillness bring order to the world.

Evolved Individuals never push anything into an extreme state — not even positive
achievements — because they know when things are too full, they cannot be used
effectively. Only when a cup is empty is it at its most useful; only when an accomplishment is open-ended does it continue to grow. Lao Tzu believed that the world
would become naturally organized and useful if extremes were avoided and insights
cultivated into the laws of nature.

    In this passage, the "cold" that is overcome by agitation refers to inanimate,
nonliving things that need vigorous action to transform them into useful tools for
humans. The "heated" that is overcome by stillness refers to humans, who require
centeredness and clarity to evolve into useful contributors to the collective awareness
of the world.

躁勝寒。靜勝熱。清靜爲天下正

大直若屈。大巧若拙。大辯若訥

大成若缺。其用不弊。大盈若沖。其用不窮

LAO TZU RIDING ON A BUFFALO

From the Chung Kuo Ku Tai Pan Hua Ts'ung K'an

KNOWING ENOUGH

When the world possesses the Tao,
    Even fast horses are used for their dung.
When the world is without the Tao,
    War-horses are raised in the suburbs.

There is no greater misfortune
    Than not knowing what is enough.
There is no greater fault
    Than desiring to acquire.

Therefore know that enough is enough.
There will always be enough.

Lao Tzu believed that the gravest character flaw, especially in leaders since they influence people and lead organizations, is acquisitiveness. Leaders who are acquisitive are looking for the meaning of life outside of themselves. Therefore their inner life develops no purpose or substance. When an organization is led in accord with the Tao — when it does not act in an acquisitive fashion toward other organizations — then even its greatest advantages are used for cultivating the internal quality of the organization (fast horses are used for their dung). Conversely, when an organization is not led in accord with the Tao — when it engages in acquisitive conduct toward other organizations — then its advantages are used aggressively outside the organization and the people must pay for this (war-horses are raised in the suburbs). Organizations in accord with the Tao know what is enough. For this reason, they attain freedom, power, and independence.

故知足之足。常足矣

禍莫大。於不知足。咎莫大。於欲得

天下有道。卻走馬以糞。天下無道。戎馬生於郊

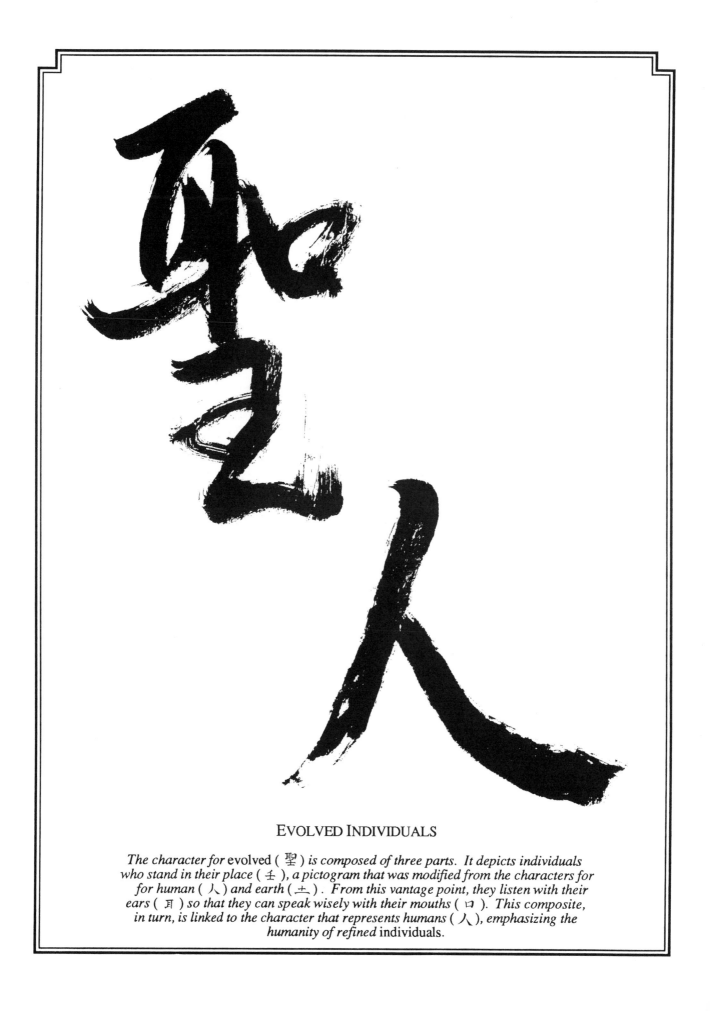

EVOLVED INDIVIDUALS

The character for evolved (聖) is composed of three parts. It depicts individuals who stand in their place (壬), a pictogram that was modified from the characters for for human (人) and earth (土). From this vantage point, they listen with their ears (耳) so that they can speak wisely with their mouths (口). This composite, in turn, is linked to the character that represents humans (人), emphasizing the humanity of refined individuals.

CULTIVATING INNER-KNOWLEDGE

Without going out of doors,
    Know the world.
Without looking through the window,
    See the Tao in Nature.
One may travel very far,
    And know very little.

Therefore, Evolved Individuals
    Know without going about,
    Recognize without looking,
    Achieve without acting.

The most valuable knowledge one can acquire comes through the cultivation of intuition and the practice of noninterference. This knowledge addresses a deeper level of awareness than that gained through action, for knowledge that comes through action is obscured by situation-specific reactions. Those who follow the Tao use strategic noninterference to lead them to exceptional awareness. In this way Evolved Individuals can align themselves so that their inner world reflects the world around them. They are using tactical inertness to ensure that their current instincts and impressions are in harmony with the larger forces at work in the world. With this knowledge they can position themselves appropriately and effectively in order to achieve their aims.

NONACTION

The character for action (爲) *is from the ancient pictogram of a female monkey with a human body, scratching her head (禺). It was modified to represent a hand (⺤) combing strands of fibers (爪) to prepare them for the loom. To indicate* nonaction, *this character is combined with one meaning "no more" (無). Originally, this was a pictogram of a luxuriant forest (林) destroyed by a large number (卅) of people (人).*

THE ART OF NONACTION

To pursue the academic, add to it daily.
To pursue the Tao, subtract from it daily.
Subtract and subtract again,
To arrive at nonaction.
Through nonaction nothing is left undone.

The world is always held without effort.
The moment there is effort,
The world is beyond holding.

This passage is a thought experiment that explores the practice of calculated non-action as the means to gain powerful insights into worldly affairs. Those who follow the Tao are concerned with removing fixed ideas from the mind in order to clear the way for impressions based on the transformation and evolution of their environment. Static information limits the mind's ability to "read" impressions that are coming into it in the language of possibility and change. Lao Tzu believed that using action or effort to elicit information would yield a contaminated form of reality — one based on the world's reactions to one's actions. The Taoist ideal is to gain pure information by observing a world that is not reacting to one's interference. Evolved Individuals use pure information to refine their intuitive and instinctive knowledge.

The word *academic* may also be translated as "study" or "learning."
It refers to information that comes through rote learning or
imitation.

取天下常以無事。及其有事。不足以取天下

無為而無不為

為學日益。為道日損。損之又損。以至於無為。

INFANT

Infant (孩) *was originally an ideogram depicting a child with legs and arms outstretched (* 兒 *). This was later modified to show a swaddled child with arms reaching out (* 子 *). It is combined with a phonetic modifier (* 亥 *), which represents the hours from 9 to 11 p.m., the most propitious time of day for conception.*

OPENING THE MIND

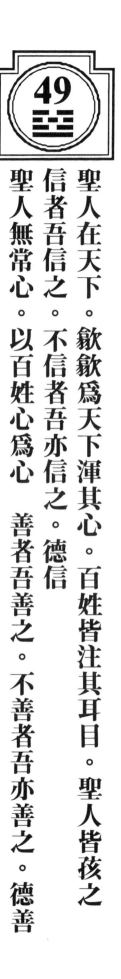

Evolved Individuals have no fixed mind;
They make the mind of the People their mind.

To those who are good, I am good;
    To those who are not good, I am also good.
Goodness is Power.

Of those who trust, I am trusting;
    Of those who do not trust, I am also trusting.
Trust is Power.

The Evolved Individuals in the world
    Attract the world and merge with its mind.
The People all focus their eyes and ears;
    Evolved Individuals all act as infants.

Evolved Individuals keep their minds open and impartial because fixed opinions or belief systems distort the flow of pure information coming in from the outside world. They enhance their understanding of the world and their position in it by merging with the collective mind of world society. They do not rely solely on information gained through their eyes and ears, but look beyond with an open heart and mind. In this way, infantlike, they can act upon the world without unbalancing it.

    By trusting those who cannot find trust in themselves and showing goodness to those who are not good people, Evolved Individuals are emulating the Tao. They are using an opposite force to neutralize an extreme, thus altering the internal reality of untrusting, mean people. This response runs contrary to the common one where aggression is met with aggression, hate with hate, and anger with anger. In observing the laws of nature, however, Evolved Individuals realize that an acid is not neutralized by adding more acid. It is neutralized by infusing it with its opposite: an alkaline solution. Lao Tzu believed that the ability to neutralize extremes and alter reality is the ultimate Power that will bring peace to the world.

In this passage, the word *People* can be literally translated as "the hundred families." This term refers to all of the family names in China and represents the entire population.

THE ART OF SURVIVAL

As life goes out, death comes in.

Life has thirteen paths;
    Death has thirteen paths.
Human life arrives at the realm of death
    Also in thirteen moves.

Why is this so?
Because life is lived lavishly.

Now, as it is well known,
    Those skilled in attracting life
Can travel across the land
    And not meet a rhinoceros or tiger.
When the military comes in,
    Their defense cannot be attacked.

The rhinoceros is without a place to thrust its horn.
The tiger is without a place to affix its claw.
The military is without a place to admit its blade.

Why is this so?
Because they are without the realm of death.

The thirteen paths mentioned in this passage are the human senses and their apertures. These are carefully monitored and controlled in Evolved Individuals, who practice moderation and limit sensory input to levels where more energy is coming in than going out. They know that the life force grows stronger when the energy received from the senses is spent on internal growth. A strong life force creates certain invulnerabilities in life. Lao Tzu believed that individuals are protected from harm, not because they are lucky, but because they do not cultivate weaknesses (the realm of death). Therefore, Evolved Individuals do not put themselves into positions where they are vulnerable to attack or misfortune. They are aware that as life goes out death comes in, so they preserve their energy and engage in life-enhancing pursuits.

The significance of the number 13 in this passage comes from the nine orifices and four limbs of humans, each likely to attract life as well as death.

出生入死

生之徒十有三。死之徒十有三。人之生動之死地。亦十有三

夫何故？以其生生之厚

蓋聞。善攝生者。陸行。不遇兕虎。入軍。不被甲兵

兕無所投其角。虎無所措其爪。兵無所容其刃

夫何故？以其無死地

POWER

The character for power (德) *has several elements. The first part (彳) indicates a step forward. The second part is made up of straightness (一) that ten (十) eyes (罒) can find no fault with. This is positioned over the symbol for a beating heart (心), which is derived from an actual representation of the organ (ㅂ) with the aorta descending below it (屮).*

THE POWER OF IMPARTIAL SUPPORT

The Tao produces;
    Its Power supports;
Its Natural Law forms;
    Its influence completes.

Thus All Things without exception
    Respect the Tao and value its Power.
To respect the Tao and value its Power —
    No one demands this, and it comes naturally.

Therefore the Tao produces and its Power supports;
It advances, cultivates, comforts, matures, nourishes, and protects.

Produce but do not possess.
Act without expectation.
Advance without dominating.
These are called the Subtle Powers.

The Tao is indifferent to that which it produces, but its movements tend to support those who follow a natural and spontaneous path. Furthermore, its Power (*Te*) can be used by those who align themselves with its current influence. For those who do not use the Tao — who work against the grain of their own natures and against the Natural Laws — the Tao remains, as always, indifferent. The only result of such action, for individuals so engaged, is a difficult life path.

    In the East, the universe is generally regarded as illusory, and the source behind it — the Absolute — is viewed as impersonal: an intelligence merely creating and supporting matter and energy for its own manifestation. Therefore, in the Eastern view, individuals who maintain an attitude of impartiality, in emulation of the laws of nature, are able to use the Subtle Powers to shape their own destiny.

長之育之亭之毒之養之覆之　生而不有。爲而不恃。長而不宰。是謂玄德。

道之尊德之貴。夫莫之命而常自然　故道生之德畜之。

道生之。德畜之。物形之。勢成之　是以萬物莫不。尊道而貴德。

RETURNING TO INSIGHT

The beginning of the world
May be regarded as the Mother of the world.
To apprehend the Mother,
Know the offspring.
To know the offspring
Is to remain close to the Mother,
And free from harm throughout life.

Block the passages,
        Close the doors;
                In the end, life is idle.

Open the passages,
        Increase undertakings;
                In the end, life is hopeless.

To perceive the small is called insight.
To remain yielding is called strength.
If, in using one's brightness,
One returns to insight,
Life will be free of misfortune.

This is called learning the Absolute.

The term *Mother* is another expression used in the *Tao Te Ching* to describe the Tao. Her offspring are the "ten thousand things": All Things in the universe. Here it is suggested that by observing the physical laws that govern the behavior of matter, one can begin to perceive the Tao. When one knows the Tao, life holds less fear, for the mind expands and becomes familiar with the unknown.

In this passage, two approaches to the outside world are described. In one, individuals close down their senses and cut off external input; in the other, individuals open wide all their senses and lose themselves in worldly endeavors. Both approaches have less-than-fortunate results: one lacks meaningful undertakings, the other is hopelessly entangled. Instead Lao Tzu presents a strategy to lend stability to worldly perceptions and avert difficulties. By continually augmenting one's external view of the the world with information from the intuitive mind, one develops a sense of the continuous processes and patterns in life. This cultivation of instinct and intuition is indispensable to the development of an evolved mind.

天下有始。以爲天下母。

既得其母。以知其子。

既知其子。復守其母。沒身不殆

塞其兌。閉其門。終身不勤

開其兌。濟其事。終身不救 見小曰明。守柔曰强。

用其光。復歸其明。無遺身殃 是謂習常

THE EMPEROR T'AI TSUNG

The Emperor T'ai Tsung (A.D. 597-649), whose personal name was Li Shih-min, was the second son of the Emperor Kao Tsu, founder of the T'ang Dynasty. He helped his father topple the dying Sui Dynasty, whose grandiose ambition to militarily unify China and construct a superior canal system had taxed the people into poverty. When his father took the reins of the empire, T'ai Tsung took an active part in social reforms. T'ai Tsung fostered education and restored astronomy to a practical, rather than metaphysical, science. Upon his father's retirement he embarked on a reign of unparalleled brilliance.

Emperor T'ai Tsung learned from the lesson of the corrupt Sui Dynasty. He gave power to educated civil servants rather than aristocrats or military officers, and encouraged his courtiers to express themselves freely. He frequently summoned local officials to inquire into the well-being of his subjects and continuously reviewed the policies of his government. In later years he wrote the book A Guide for Emperors to pass on to his descendants; and among his recorded sayings, the best known is: "By using a mirror of brass, you may see to adjust your cap; by using antiquity as a mirror, you may learn to foresee the rise and fall of empires."

The National Palace Museum, Taipei, Taiwan

THE UNDIVIDED PATH

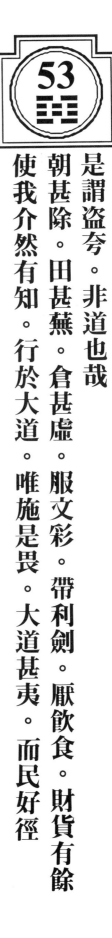

Using only a little knowledge,
I would travel the Great Way
And fear only of letting go.
The Great Way is very even;
Yet people love the byways.

When an organization is divided,
     Fields are overgrown,
     Stores are empty,
     Clothes are extravagant,
     Sharp swords are worn,
     Food and drink are excessive,
     Wealth and treasure are hoarded.

This is called stealing and exaggeration
And certainly not the Way!

Following the Great Way — the Tao — requires no special knowledge or learning; it is merely listening to the inner voice, taking note of the current social and environmental patterns, and holding to the path of least resistance. The path of least resistance is level and even, but for many the bypaths are tempting. The bypaths, in the social realm, are excessive ambitions and desires that divide people from their inner natures and from one another. When individuals indulge in extremes it serves only to block their own personal development; but when organizations act this way, there is danger to both the people whom they serve and to the organizations themselves.

    A divided organization is one that is acting ambitiously or aggressively toward its people or toward other organizations. These organizations economize where they should spend (on nurturing and support) and spend where they should economize (on appearances and weapons). Unbalanced organizations act against the laws of nature, and thus they cannot remain long on earth.

ESTABLISHING A UNIVERSAL VIEW

What is skillfully established will not be uprooted;
What is skillfully grasped will not slip away.
Thus it is honored for generations.

Cultivate the inner self;
    Its Power becomes real.
Cultivate the home;
    Its Power becomes abundant.
Cultivate the community;
    Its Power becomes greater.
Cultivate the organization;
    Its Power becomes prolific.
Cultivate the world;
    Its Power becomes universal.

Therefore through the inner self,
    The inner self is conceived.
Through the home,
    The home is conceived.
Through the community,
    The community is conceived.
Through the organization,
    The organization is conceived.
Through the world,
    The world is conceived.

How do I know the world?
Through this.

This passage describes a global perspective used to gain insight into the interdependent relationship between the individual and the outside world. Beginning with the smallest social unit, the self, and then continuing on to the family, the community, its governing body, and world society, wherever Taoist principles are applied, intelligent energy is enhanced. But in order to align those social units to the Tao, their underlying patterns must be perceived by constructing in the mind a vision of an ideally operating social unit: one that functions in a noncontentious, appropriately supportive, and socially aesthetic manner. In order to conceive of an ideally functioning world, Evolved Individuals cultivate the inner mind. The power of a world vision in an evolved mind can help draw that ideal into reality for future generations.

善建者不拔。善抱者不脫。子孫以祭祀不輟

修之於身。其德乃眞。修之於家。其德乃餘。修之於鄉。

其德乃長。修之於國。其德乃豐。修之天下。其德乃普

故以身觀身。以家觀家。以鄉觀鄉。

以國觀國。以天下觀天下

吾何以知天下然哉？以此

THE POWER IN NOT CONTENDING

To possess Power that runs deep
Is to be like a newborn child.

Poisonous insects do not sting it,
    Fierce beasts do not seize it,
        Birds of prey do not strike it.

Its bones are yielding,
    Its muscles are relaxed,
        Its grip is strong.

It does not yet know the union of male and female,
    Yet its virility is active.
        Its Life Force is at its greatest.

It can scream all day,
    Yet it does not become hoarse.
        Its Harmony is at its greatest.

To know Harmony is called the Absolute.
To know the Absolute is called insight.
To enhance life is called propitious.
To be conscious of Influence is called strength.

Things overgrown must decline.
This is not the Tao.
What is not the Tao will soon end.

The infant is a frequent metaphor in the *Tao Te Ching*. To be infantlike is to be in touch both with one's original nature and the current reality in the environment. Infants act and react appropriately and spontaneously and do not attack or contend; thus they are protected. Evolved Individuals, therefore, use spontaneity and non-contention as a spiritual martial art to transcend social dangers. When they are pushed, they yield, and the pushers are thrown off balance by their own inappropriate efforts. Evolved Individuals focus solely on maintaining their stability and balance — a position that yields power. The physical laws of the universe reflect the fact that unbalanced energies are not stable and their time as such quickly passes.

55

含德之厚。比於赤子

毒蟲不螫。猛獸不據。攫鳥不搏

骨弱。筋柔。而握固　未知牝牡之合。而峻作。精之至也

終日號。而不嗄。和之至也

知和曰常。知常曰明。益生曰祥。心使氣曰強

物壯則老。謂之不道。不道早已

LAO TZU RIDING AN OX

The Cleveland Museum of Art, Cleveland, Ohio

GAINING ONENESS

Those who know do not speak.
Those who speak do not know.

Block the passages.
Close the door.
Blunt the sharpness.
Untie the tangles.
Harmonize the brightness.
Identify with the ways of the world.

This is called Profound Identification.

It cannot be gained through attachment.
It cannot be gained through detachment.
It cannot be gained through advantage.
It cannot be gained through disadvantage.
It cannot be gained through esteem.
It cannot be gained through humility.

Hence it is the treasure of the world.

The first two lines of this passage are among the most quoted from the *Tao Te Ching*. Lao Tzu suggests that if one's understanding of the world is based primarily on a teaching that comes from outside the inner mind, then it is not a natural structure of the physical universe, but is instead a temporary structure of the culture. As such, it can be of no use to those who follow the Tao, since they rely upon the impressions of the intuitive mind, which evolves and changes along with the universe.

   In order to cultivate the inner mind, those who follow the Tao engage in thought experiments that unleash the intuitive powers and promote intellectual independence. Evolved Individuals control external input, neutralize aggression, simplify their plans and strategies, and put their awareness in harmony with social and environmental patterns. In other words, they achieve oneness with the unfolding universe: Profound Identification. Because this state of mind cannot be reached through social or intellectual strategies, individuals who achieve this state in turn cannot be used or coerced. They have achieved personal power through incorruptible simplicity and inner truth.

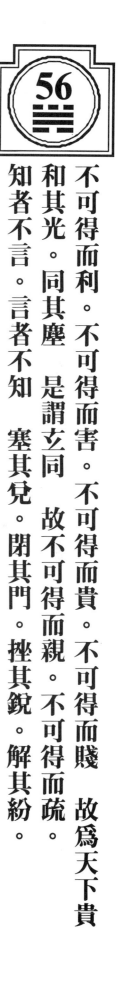

不可得而利。不可得而害。不可得而貴。不可得而賤　故爲天下貴

和其光。同其塵　是謂玄同　故不可得而親。不可得而疏。

知者不言。言者不知　塞其兌。閉其門。挫其銳。解其紛。

THE POWER IN EFFORTLESSNESS

Lead the organization with correctness.
Direct the military with surprise tactics.
Take hold of the world with effortlessness.

How do I know it is so?
Through this:

Too many prohibitions in the world,
    And people become insufficient.
Too many sharp weapons among people,
    And the nation grows confused.
Too much cunning strategy among people,
    And strange things start to happen.
Too obvious a growth in laws and regulations,
    And too many criminals emerge.

Thus Evolved Individuals say:

Look to nonaction,
    And people will be naturally influenced.
Look to refined tranquillity,
    And people will be naturally correct.
Look to effortlessness,
    And people will be naturally affluent.
Look to nondesire,
    And people will be naturally simple.

In this passage Lao Tzu suggests that leaders might unite the world if they could lead without interference and govern without restrictive social structures. Too many controls and regulations are a form of aggression against the natural processes of refinement in people. In the Taoist view, the instincts of humans are fair and correct and become aggressive and cunning only in reaction to excessive force from restrictive laws and imposed morality. Leaders who rise up and attempt to repress or manipulate others — collectively or individually — ultimately achieve the opposite of their aims. Such force defeats itself and in the process leads the organization into chaos.

Evolved Leaders reverse this process. They do not interfere when they can avoid it; they are a model of intelligent calm within the organization; they undertake endeavors where they are easy and nonconfrontive; and they subdue in their hearts ostentatious ambitions and irrelevant desires. As a result, the people are favorably influenced; they conduct themselves appropriately; they naturally prosper; and they do not indulge in complex strategies and intrigues. In this way they naturally unite.

以正治國。以奇用兵。以無事取天下

吾何以知其然哉？以此　天下多忌諱。而民彌貧。

民多利器。國家滋昏。人多伎巧。奇物滋起。法令滋彰。

盜賊多有　故聖人云　我無爲。而民自化。

我好靜。而民自正。我無事。

而民自富。我無欲。而民自樸

BRIGHT

The character for bright (光), *written in its ancient form* (苂), *is a combination of the symbols for twenty* (廿) *fires* (火). *In more recent times, the character depicts a person* (儿) *carrying a torch* (火) *overhead for illumination.*

CULTIVATING THE CENTER

If the administration is subdued,
    The people are sincere.
        If the administration is exacting,
            The people are deficient.

Misfortune! Good fortune supports it.
    Good Fortune! Misfortune hides within.
        Who knows where it ends?
            Is there no order?

Order can revert to the unusual;
    Good can revert to the abnormal;
        And people indeed are bewildered
            For a long, long time.

Thus Evolved Individuals are
    Square without dividing;
    Honest without offending;
    Straightforward without straining;
    Bright without dazzling.

Severe controls and regulations characterize a detailed and exacting administration. Such an administration conceives of an ideal subject and then attempts to regulate the people into this ideal. Since human nature invariably resists repression, resentment and discontent begin to grow within the organization. As the administration pushes, the resistance of the people grows even stronger. Evolved Leaders understand the action of polarity in nature, and therefore they avoid such extremes. They know that misfortune and good fortune do not respond to direct control, and that excessive regulations toward "good" and "order" will surely cause a counter-reaction. Instead they use their intelligence to shape the world without direct confrontation or excessive strategy or control. Stable, subtle, and sincere, they cultivate themselves and become models for their subjects.

58

其政悶悶。其民淳淳。其政察察。其民缺缺　禍兮福之所倚。

其日固久　是以聖人。方而不割。廉而不劌。直而不肆。光而不耀

福兮禍之所伏。孰知其極？其無正？正復爲奇。善復爲妖。人之迷。

MOTHER

Mother (母) *is composed of the ancient pictogram of a woman in the traditional Chinese childbearing pose (* 🈀 *). It was later altered to the more current character for woman (* 女 *) to make it easier to write. The addition to this character of two dots for breasts (* ⺀ *) indicates a woman who suckles her offspring, a mother.*

THE WAY OF MODERATION

In leading people and serving Nature,
    There is nothing better than moderation.
Since, indeed, moderation means yielding early;
    Yielding early means accumulating Power.

When Power is accumulated,
    Nothing is impossible.
When nothing is impossible,
    One knows no limits.
One who knows no limits
    Can possess the organization.

An organization that possesses the Mother
    Can endure and advance.
This means deep roots and firm foundation:
    Durability and longevity through observation of the Tao.

The responsibility of Evolved Leaders is to guide their subjects effectively while remaining centered and self-aware; this is what is meant by "serving Nature." To achieve moderation, leaders scrupulously avoid extremes and adopt nonconfrontive postures. With moderation comes endurance, personal power, and unlimited possibilities. Centered leaders tend to experience an ever-expanding influence. When Evolved Leaders, in turn, structure their organization in accord with the moderate, centered path of the Tao, it will not be eroded by the turbulence of the extremes and will therefore enjoy a long and prosperous existence.

The term *Mother* refers to the Tao. It is used as a metaphor since the Tao, like the Mother, is the originator of all events.

治人事天。莫如嗇。夫唯嗇是謂早服。早服謂之重積德

重積德。則無不克。無不克。則莫知其極。莫知其極。可以有國

有國之母。可以長久。是謂深根固柢。長生久視之道

EMPEROR KAO TSU OF THE T'ANG DYNASTY

The Emperor Kao Tsu, whose given name was Li Yuan (A.D. 565-635), was a commandant at the end of the corrupt Sui Dynasty. The Sui Dynasty had exacted a great toll on the Chinese people in the form of high taxes and forced labor, and its unpopularity weakened its stability. With the aid of his son, Kao Tsu set up a puppet king for the two years of dynastic upheaval that followed the popular revolt. Then Kao Tsu himself took the reins of power and ushered in China's golden era, the T'ang Dynasty.

As founder of the T'ang Dynasty, the Emperor Kao Tsu ruled from 618 to 626. He brought about reforms to expose and neutralize the political corruption of the Sui. He redistributed the land holdings among the Chinese people and instituted an "in-kind" system of taxation, whereby peasants could pay in goods or foods, thus weakening the powers of the moneyed classes. Under his leadership, China was pacified and united. After nine years he abdicated in favor of his son and took the title of Emperor Emeritus.

The National Palace Museum, Taipei, Taiwan

HOLDING THE POSITION

Leading a large organization is like cooking a small fish.

If the Tao is present in the world,
    The cunning are not mysterious.
Not only are the cunning not mysterious,
    Their mystery does not harm others.

Not only does their mystery not harm others,
    The Evolved also do not harm others.
Since together they do no harm,
    The Power returns and accumulates.

In order to support the organization in an uncertain atmosphere, a leader must emulate the Tao by "cooking a small fish" appropriately. Just as too much stirring will cause a delicate fish to fall apart, too much interference during a difficult period will unbalance the situation and one's place within it. When there are no elegant, effortless solutions, the appropriate stance is to allow the natural forces, the Tao, to evolve problems and point the way toward their resolution. Therefore, the first concern of Evolved Leaders is to cultivate the Tao in organizational affairs. Once the Tao is enlisted — through sensitive, observant noninterference — many things will become clear to everyone involved. Those who would plan cunning strategies for personal gain become obvious and thus ineffective. Once the organization needs no longer to fear internal manipulation, productivity will prevail.

The term *cunning* comes from the Chinese word *kuei.* It may also be translated as "spirit," "ghost," or "demon." *Kuei,* as spirits, are considered more mischievous and crafty than they are sinister or evil.

THE POWER IN MODESTY

A large organization should flow downward
To intersect with the world.
It is the female of the world.
The female always overcomes the male by stillness;
Through stillness, she makes herself low.

Thus if a large organization
    Is lower than a small organization,
        It can receive the small organization.
And if a small organization
    Stays lower than a large organization,
        It can receive the large organization.

Therefore one receives by becoming low;
Another receives by being low.

Yet what a large organization desires
    Is to unite and support others.
And what a small organization desires
    Is to join and serve others.

So for both to gain the position they desire,
The larger should place itself low.

A nonaggressive, noninterfering stance is the natural diplomatic position for a large, powerful organization to take toward a smaller one. This yielding position gives the impression of submission, but has the advantage of generosity. When this position is held, the small organization will not resent the power and position of the larger organization — and the large, by not aggressively promoting its own interests, will attract trust and cooperation from the smaller. Such positioning on the part of the larger organization addresses the psychological needs of both, since large organizations benefit by uniting and supporting others, and small organizations benefit by serving a larger audience. The power that comes from serving others occurs in all possible relationships — from the interpersonal to the international. The Chinese say that "to rule is to serve." A Taoist would say that "to serve is to rule."

61

大國者下流。天下之交。天下之牝。牝常以靜勝牡。

以靜爲下　故大國。以下小國。則取小國。

小國。以下大國。則取大國

故或下以取。或下而取　大國不過欲。兼畜人

小國不過欲。入事人

夫兩者各得其所欲。大者宜爲下

THE TAO IN LEADERS

The Tao is a refuge for All Things,
The treasure of the good,
The protector of the not good.

Honor can be bought with fine words;
    Others can be joined with fine conduct.
So if some are not good,
    Why waste them?

In this way the Emperor is established;
    The three officials are installed.
And although the large jade disc
    Is preceded by a team of horses,
This is not as good as sitting,
    Advancing in the Tao.

Why did those of old treasure the Tao?
Did they not say:
    Seek it and it is attained;
    Possess faults and they are released?
Thus it is the treasure of the world.

In organizations, the leader's role is to help all members find their place and direct them together into progress and fulfillment. Even though some people may be insufficient or unrefined, Lao Tzu asks, "Why waste them?" An Evolved Leader is certain to provide for the necessary education of everyone in the organization. In this way all members become integrated in the organization and the leader's position is established. To maintain that position, Evolved Leaders do not put emphasis on the material advantages and the grand appearances of leadership, for these will only serve to separate the world of the leader from the world of the people. The people's needs cannot be met by such a leader. Instead Evolved Leaders look within to sense the direction of social evolution (the Tao). In this way, they guide the people on the appropriate path and they make no mistakes.

The term *refuge (ao)* refers to the southwest corner of the house, where treasures are stored. This is a custom stemming from *feng shui*, the art of site-planning in early Chinese architecture.

道者萬物之奧。善人之寶。不善人之所保

美言可以市尊。善行可以加入。人之不善。何棄之有？

故立天子。置三公。雖有拱璧

以先駟馬。不如坐進。此道　古之所以貴此道者？

何不曰。以求得。

有罪以免邪？故爲天下貴

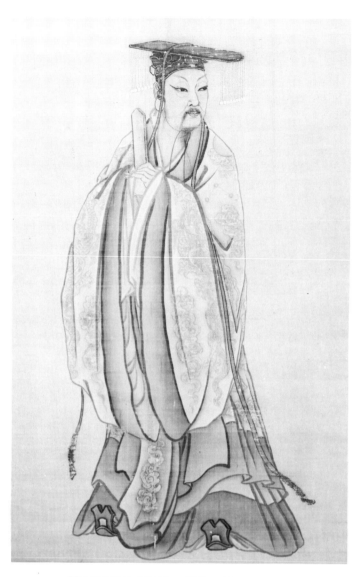

KING YU OF THE HSIA DYNASTY

During the reign of the legendary Emperor Yao, from 2357 to 2205 B.C., China was plagued by devastating seasonal floods. Emperor Yao enlisted Yu's father to oversee the control of China's rivers by building a series of dikes. He failed after nine years of effort. The next Emperor, Shun, asked Yu to continue his father's work, and Yu took on the project, but with a different approach. Instead of trying to fight the rivers, he had them dredged and channeled so they could more easily reach their goal, the sea, thereby bringing the floods under control.

To complete his work, Yu travelled throughout the countryside for thirteen years. He was so intent on his mission that he passed his home three times but never entered. He also made careful studies of the people he came across in his travels and established what their tribute to the court should be. As a reward for his distinguished services, Emperor Shun abdicated in his favor. King Yu founded the Hsia Dynasty and reigned from 2205 to 2197 B.C. To this day, King Yu's birthday, which falls on June 6, is known as Engineer's Day in China.

The National Palace Museum, Taipei, Taiwan

THE PATH OF LEAST RESISTANCE

Act without action; work without effort.
    Taste without savoring.
Magnify the small; increase the few.
    Repay ill-will with kindness.

Plan the difficult when it is easy;
    Handle the big where it is small.
The world's hardest work begins when it is easy;
    The world's largest effort begins where it is small.
Evolved Individuals, finally, take no great action,
    And in that way the great is achieved.

Those who commit easily, inspire little trust.
    How easy to inspire hardness!
Therefore Evolved Individuals view all as difficult.
    Finally they have no difficulty!

When Evolved Individuals must influence an ongoing process they will direct their energy toward its weakest and most receptive area. Once their influence is absorbed, they know that the weakness will move to another location. They follow. Never do they find themselves in a direct confrontation with a formidable problem. Just as a river finds its way through a valley of boulders, Evolved Individuals work their way around areas of resistance, knowing that they will ultimately wear them down. Thus an entire process can be influenced and controlled with small, nonconfrontive actions. Because Evolved Individuals are serious minded, they inspire trust and break down resistance; because they are subtle, their actions are appropriately restrained and do not interfere with the natural cycle of events. In this way they avoid counter-reactions and achieve their aims.

夫輕諾必寡信。多易必多難。是以聖人猶難之。故終無難矣

天下難事必作於易。天下大事必作於細。是以聖人終不爲大。故能成其大

爲無爲事無事。味無味。大小多少。報怨以德　圖難於其易。爲大於其細。

THE POWER AT THE BEGINNING

What is at rest is easy to hold;
    What is not yet begun is easy to plan.
What is thin is easy to melt;
    What is minute is easy to disperse.
Deal with things before they emerge;
    Put them in order before there is disorder.

A tree of many arm spans is produced from a tiny sprout.
A tower of nine stories is raised from a pile of earth.
A journey of a thousand miles begins with a footstep.

Those who act on things, spoil them;
    Those who seize things, lose them.
Thus Evolved Individuals do nothing;
    Hence they spoil nothing.
They seize nothing;
    Hence they lose nothing.

People often spoil their work at the point of its completion.
With care at the end as well as the beginning,
No work will be spoiled.

Thus Evolved Individuals desire to be desireless
    And do not treasure goods that are hard to get.
They learn without learning,
    By returning to the place where the Collective Mind passes.
In this way they assist All Things naturally
    Without venturing to act.

This passage explores the control that an individual might gain in worldly events through the use of strategic noninterference. The underlying principle in this idea is a very basic one in the physical sciences: Every action produces a reaction; the more forceful the action, the stronger the ultimate counter-force. Thus the results of forceful actions will either neutralize the individual doing the forcing, or they will hopelessly contaminate the situation being acted upon. For this reason, Evolved Individuals guide and control events by developing an instinct about where and when events originate. They can then act when situations are in their smallest, simplest, most unentrenched, and least reactive state — and at the same time they can position themselves to guide the situation through to completion. The instinct that signals the origins of events can be cultivated in individuals who are not blinded by excessive desires or crippled by dogmatic thinking. Individuals who are free of such limitations can use their intuitive powers to guide the world around them.

The word *miles* is a translation of the Chinese word *li*, which is actually a distance of about one-third of a mile.

64

其安易持。其未兆易謀。其脆易泮。
其微易散。爲之於未有。治之於未亂
合抱之木生於毫末。九層之臺起於累土。千里之行始於足下
爲者敗之。執者失之。是以聖人無爲。故無敗。無執。故無失
民之從事常於幾成而敗之。愼終如始　則無敗事　是以聖人欲不欲。
不貴難得之貨。學不學。復衆人之所過。以輔萬物之自然。而不敢爲

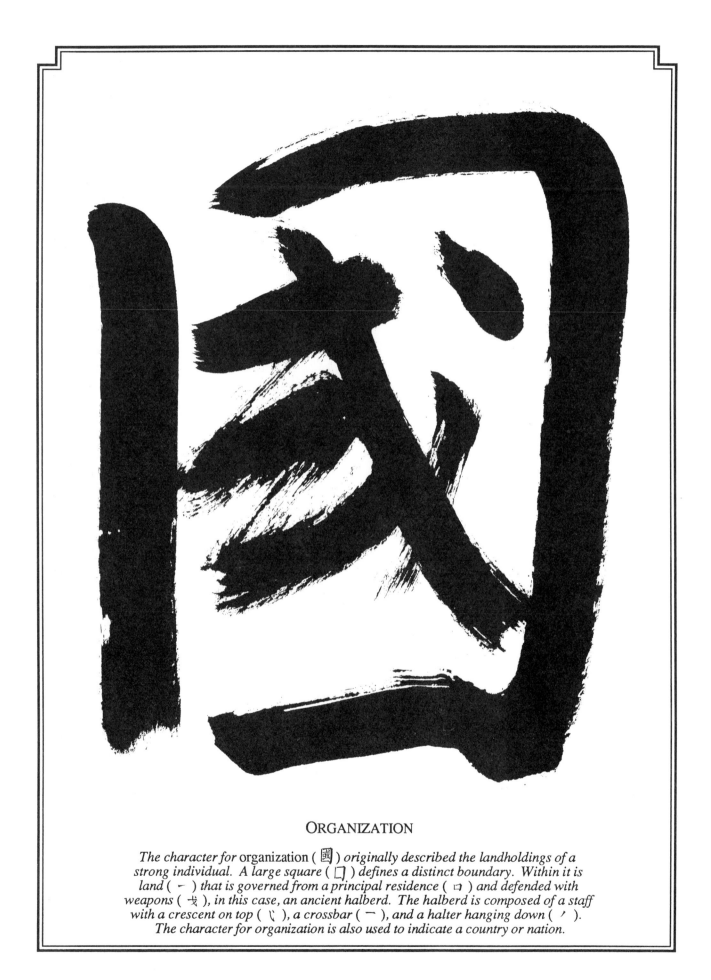

ORGANIZATION

The character for organization (國) originally described the landholdings of a strong individual. A large square (囗) defines a distinct boundary. Within it is land (一) that is governed from a principal residence (口) and defended with weapons (戈), in this case, an ancient halberd. The halberd is composed of a staff with a crescent on top (㇄), a crossbar (一), and a halter hanging down (ノ). The character for organization is also used to indicate a country or nation.

THE DANGER IN CLEVERNESS

Those skillful in the ancient Tao
Are not obvious to the people.
They appear to be simple-minded.

People are difficult to lead
    Because they are too clever.
Hence, to lead the organization with cleverness
    Will harm the organization.
To lead the organization without cleverness
    Will benefit the organization.

Those who know these two things
    Have investigated the patterns of the Absolute.
To know and investigate the patterns
    Is called the Subtle Power.

The Subtle Power is profound and far-reaching.
Together with the Natural Law of polarity,
It leads to the Great Harmony.

Leaders who impose elaborate strategies on people cause social reactions that undermine the structure of the organization because clever strategies strike a resonant chord in people and trigger their own cunning responses. If leaders, instead, guide the organization with simplicity and directness, the inherent cleverness of the people will be disarmed. Simple and direct leadership is highly effective when it is intelligently aligned with the general trends in the environment. For that reason, it is essential for leaders to examine both the current patterns in society and the constant laws in nature.

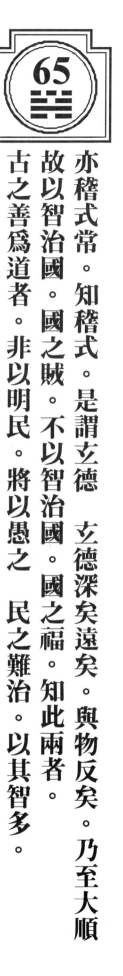

古之善爲道者。非以明民。將以愚之　民之難治。以其智多。

故以智治國。國之賊。不以智治國。國之福。知此兩者。

亦稽式常。知稽式。是謂玄德　玄德深矣遠矣。與物反矣。乃至大順

清 聖 祖 康 熙

PORTRAIT OF THE EMPEROR K'ANG HSI

The Emperor K'ang Hsi (A.D. 1655-1723) succeeded to the throne at the age of eight and took up the reins of government at fifteen. His understanding and compassionate policies endeared him to his people, and although he was personally frugal, he lavished large sums on public works. He regularly toured the empire to inquire into the welfare of his people; and during his sixty-one-year reign the empire became so peaceful and prosperous that tax payments were cancelled several times.

K'ang Hsi had a superior and inquiring mind, and his literary undertakings along with his sense of the importance of recorded history made him one of China's most illustrious leaders. He edited the vast Imperial Dictionary of over forty thousand characters and ordered the compilation of the two extensive illustrated encyclopedias of Chinese life and customs. Because he believed that cultural information would help strengthen and protect the empire, the Emperor K'ang Hsi supervised the production of a vast compendium of Chinese literature containing over ten thousand volumes.

Percival David Foundation of Chinese Art, London, England

THE POWER IN STAYING LOW

The rivers and seas lead the hundred streams
Because they are skillful at staying low.
Thus they are able to lead the hundred streams.

Therefore, to rise above people,
    One must, in speaking, stay below them.
To remain in front of people,
    One must put oneself behind them.

Therefore Evolved Individuals remain above,
    And yet the people are not weighted down.
They remain in front,
    And the people are not held back.

Therefore the world willingly elects them,
    And yet it does not reject them.
Because they do not compete,
    The world cannot compete with them.

In this passage, Lao Tzu states a democratic ideal that is far more acceptable today
than it was in China twenty-five-hundred years ago. Evolved Leaders win the trust
and support of the people through their complete identification with them. The interests of the people are naturally promoted because they become the interests of the
leader as well. When it is clear in their words and actions that leaders do not feel
superior to those whom they lead, the people see themselves in their leaders and
never tire of them.

江海所以能爲百谷王者。以其善下之。故能爲百谷王　是以欲上民。必以言下之。欲先民。必以身後之　是以聖人處上。而民不重。處前。而民不害　是以天下樂推。而不厭。以其不爭。故天下莫能與之爭

THE POWER IN COMPASSION

All the world thinks that my Tao is great;
And yet it seems inconceivable.
Only its greatness makes it seem inconceivable.
If it could be conceived of,
It would have become insignificant long ago.

I have Three Treasures that support and protect:
    The first is compassion.
    The second is moderation.
    The third is daring not to be first in the world.

With compassion one becomes courageous;
    With moderation one becomes expansive.
In daring not to be first in the world,
    One becomes the instrument of leadership.

Now if one is courageous without compassion,
    Or expansive without moderation,
Or first without holding back,
    One is doomed!

Compassion always triumphs when attacked;
    It brings security when maintained.
Nature aids its leaders
    By arming them with compassion.

The Three Treasures — compassion, moderation, and the courage not to be first in the world — are the emotional foundations of Lao Tzu's method. Leaders whose position will endure are those who are the most compassionate. Compassion is a mysterious intellectual force that allows reality to act on the mind in a deeply affecting way; and in turn the mind may act upon reality. Compassionate leaders are able to make decisions with foresight and vision. Thus they triumph.

    Lao Tzu opens this passage with a paradox — the idea that something can be so large, so ever-present, and so profound that it becomes inconceivable. He suggests that anything that can be fully conceived of and acted upon by the mind becomes small and manageable. Yet true Power does not come from controlling the small and manageable. Power comes from the mind-expanding exercise of conceiving of the inconceivable.

The word *nature* can also be translated as "heaven." It refers to the external reality that appears to operate independently of humankind.

67

天下皆謂我道大。似不肖。

夫唯大故似不肖。若肖。久矣其細也

夫我有三寶持而保之。一曰慈。二曰儉。三曰不敢爲天下先

慈故能勇。儉故能廣。不敢爲天下先。故能成器長

今舍慈且勇。舍儉且廣。舍後且先。死矣

夫慈以戰則勝。以守則固。天將救之。以慈衞之

LAO TZU

The name Lao Tzu *consists of the characters for old (老) and infant (子). The character for Lao shows a person (人) whose hair and beard (毛) have changed (匕). Tzu was originally drawn as a child with its arms and legs outstretched ( ) but was later modified to a swaddled child lying on its side (子).*

NONAGGRESSIVE STRENGTH

A skillful leader does not use force.
A skillful fighter does not feel anger.
A skillful master does not engage the opponent.
A skillful employer remains low.

This is called the power in not contending.
This is called the strength to employ others.
This is called the highest emulation of Nature.

Lao Tzu believed that the most capable and ultimately the most powerful leaders are those who practice humility, subtlety, and composure. They are not aggressive and do not feel the need to prove themselves again and again. The power in composure and the strength in compassion will allow skillful leaders to organize others and achieve a collective end without the overt use of means. Therefore events unfold naturally, without disruptive counter-reactions.

PORTRAIT OF LAO TZU INSCRIBED ON STONE

NEUTRALIZING ESCALATION

The strategists have a saying:
    "I dare not act as a host,
    Yet I act as a guest.
    I dare not advance an inch,
    Yet I retreat a foot."

This is called
    Traveling without moving,
    Rising up without arms,
    Projecting without resistance,
    Capturing without strategies.

No misfortune is greater than underestimating resistance;
    Underestimating resistance will destroy my Treasures.
Thus when mutually opposing strategies escalate,
    The one who feels sorrow will triumph.

Lao Tzu viewed the clash of ideologies as a fact of social evolution, but he observed, also, that some ideologies make inroads into the minds of people, while others cause disastrous counter-reactions. He realized that resistance to ideas can be overcome — but only when indirect methods are employed will there be a lasting effect. He called this "capturing without strategies." That is why his strategist would rather "retreat a foot" than "advance an inch." Conversely, when an aggression is used to impose an ideology on others, the reaction is also a direct one: Strategy is met with strategy; weapon is matched against weapon; tensions escalate and escalate again. Lao Tzu dreaded this familiar pattern and lamented, "Underestimating resistance will destroy my Treasures." He was referring to his Three Treasures: compassion, moderation, and the courage not to be first in the world. How can escalation be neutralized? Lao Tzu believed that the side that is so socially evolved that it would experience grief over the situation would be the side whose ideology would ultimately triumph.

禍莫大於輕敵。輕敵幾喪吾寶。故抗兵相加。哀者勝矣

是謂行無行。攘無臂。扔無敵。執無兵

用兵有言。吾不敢爲主。而爲客。不敢進寸。而退尺

KNOW

The character for know (知) is a variant of the ancient pictogram for an arrow (矢) combined with the pictogram for mouth (口). It implies that people with knowledge might use their mouths with the precision of an arrow to achieve results.

KNOWING THE TAO

My words are very easy to know,
    Very easy to follow.
Yet the world is unable to know them,
    Unable to follow them.

My words have a source,
    My efforts have mastery.
Indeed, since none know this,
    They do not know me.
The rare ones who know me
    Must treasure me.

Therefore, Evolved Individuals
    Wear a coarse cloth covering
    With precious jade at the center.

Lao Tzu's philosophy is remarkable in that it stubbornly resists logical analysis, yet will readily submit to intuitive understanding. In this passage, he speaks directly to the reader using the voice of the Tao. In early China, only the ruling class and their scholars were able to read, so Lao Tzu was quite certain of his audience. He seems to assume that his readers would not have the book in their hands had they not been selected to influence the world. He hoped to instill in the minds of leaders an intuitive knowing that would allow them to peer into the future and perceive the evolution of society. He believed this would give them the power to become more compassionately understanding of themselves and their people.

For the few who do understand his words, Lao Tzu passes on one of his most important strategies for leaders. He suggests that they surround their advantages with simplicity: "a coarse cloth covering." Those who follow the Tao introduce simplicity into their lives by releasing themselves from the bondage of materialism and the discipline of elaborate social strategies. They experience high levels of personal freedom and intellectual independence and in this way they continually renew their intuitive advantage: the "precious jade at the center."

知我者希。則我者貴　是以聖人。被褐。懷玉
言有宗。事有君。夫唯無知。是以不我知。
吾言甚易知。甚易行。天下莫能知。莫能行

DISEASE

The character for disease (病) *is made up of several elements. The first part was originally a tree divided down the middle (米), the left side (爿) of which is thick and strong enough to be a bed. An individual lies (一) on this bed suffering from a fever (丙), a modification of the ideograms for fire (火) in the house (宀).*

KNOWING THE DISEASE

To know that you do not know is best.
To not know of knowing is a disease.

Indeed, to be sick of the disease,
Is the way to be free of the disease.

Evolved Individuals are free of the disease.
Because they are sick of the disease

This is the way to be free of disease.

Evolved Individuals are always aware that there is something they do not know. In the Taoist view, it is considered a great misfortune to be unconscious of one's ignorance, whether in worldly matters, interpersonal affairs, or within the self. Those who are developing personal power learn to recognize an ever-evolving universe of information that they have yet to experience. This attitude is paramount in the personal development of Evolved Individuals. It frees them from the decline that comes from being too full and too complete to grow further.

THE HSIAO T'ZU KAO EMPRESS MA

The Empress Ma (A.D. 1332-1382) and her husband, Emperor T'ai Tsu, were the founders of the Ming Dynasty. Their phenomenal rise from paupers to founders of a great empire has no parallel in Chinese history. The times were unique in that the rise of the Ming Dynasty restored Chinese rule after a century of Mongol domination. The Emperor T'ai Tsu had an intimate understanding of the needs of the common people and concentrated more power than any other monarch in Chinese history. He led the way to the restoration of Chinese culture and set about rebuilding China's bridges, temples, gardens, and walled cities.

The Empress Ma had the reputation of a devoted wife and confidant to her husband. She was considered wise, kind, and just; and perhaps in reaction to her background as a commoner, she refused to have any official titles awarded to her relatives, except for the title of prince for her late father. Her concerns were for those around her, and she constantly sought to moderate the Emperor's passionate temper. When the Emperor asked her last wishes on her deathbed, she is said to have replied: "That Your Majesty would strive for what is good, accept reproof, and be as careful at the end as at the beginning."

The National Palace Museum, Taipei, Taiwan

THE APPROPRIATE PERSPECTIVE

If the people do not fear authority,
        Then authority will expand.
Do not disrespect their position;
        Do not reject their lives.
Since, indeed, they are not rejected,
        They do not reject.

Therefore Evolved Individuals know themselves
        But do not display themselves.
They love themselves
        But do not treasure themselves.

Hence they discard one and receive the other.

Evolved Leaders are encouraged, in this passage, to minimize the distance between
their sense of their own position and the position of those whom they lead. In this
way the psychological needs of the people are better understood, and the decisions
of leaders are more aligned with those needs. Lao Tzu believed that the less people
fear or focus upon the embodiment of authority, the more effective authority becomes. In order to develop and preserve this appropriate attitude, leaders should
closely identify with those whom they lead. When they do not exhibit and enhance
their higher position, they will discover self-knowledge. Moreover, by discarding
any sense of self-importance they may have, they will find self-love and inner peace.

NATURE

Nature (天) is depicted by the character for heaven. The human form
standing (人) with its arms outstretched (大) is defining its place in the universe.
Above and superior to the human form (一) is the greater force of the cosmos,
which refines and controls the rhythms of life.

NATURE'S WAY

Those bold in daring will die;
    Those bold in not daring will survive.
        Of these two, either may benefit or harm.

Nature decides which is evil,
    But who can know why?
        Even Evolved Individuals regard this as difficult.

The Tao in Nature
    Does not contend,
        Yet skillfully triumphs.
    Does not speak,
        Yet skillfully responds.
    Does not summon,
        And yet attracts.
    Does not hasten,
        Yet skillfully designs.

Nature's network is vast, so vast.
Its mesh is coarse, yet nothing slips through.

In the Taoist view, the way of nature is considered the ideal in behavior; it is a pattern to be followed in order to place an individual on the path of least resistance, in step with the Tao. In this passage, nature is described as an infinite network — a unified field of physical laws — that influences all actions, all thoughts, and all natural phenomena. Nothing escapes the laws of nature, and nothing escapes nature's notice and reaction. The Tao in Nature is intelligent and powerful. It achieves its plan without effort, and it responds to potentially unbalancing extremes with precision and accuracy.

73

勇於敢則殺。勇於不敢則活。此兩者或利或害
天之所惡。孰知其故？是以聖人猶難之　天之道。不爭而善勝。
不言而善應。不召而自來。繟然而善謀　天網恢恢。疏而不失

LAO TZU RIDING AN OX

The National Palace Museum, Taipei, Taiwan

UNNATURAL AUTHORITY

When people do not fear death,
How can they be threatened with death?
Suppose people fear death and still do not conform.
Who would dare seize them and put them to death?

There is always the Master Executioner who kills.
To substitute for the Master Executioner in killing
Is like substituting for the Master Carpenter who carves.
Whoever substitutes for the Master Carpenter in carving,
Rarely escapes injury to his hands.

Lao Tzu believed that people are inherently good-hearted, and that to maintain this state they require personal freedom, intellectual independence, and, most important, a life that is free of interference from above. When the organizational structures in which people live and work become oppressive, then people will no longer fear death as they reach for freedom.

The images of the Master Executioner and the Master Carpenter in this passage refer to the laws in nature that override all temporary social systems. In the Taoist view, to kill a human being — within the law or outside of it — is an unnatural act that ultimately tears apart the fabric of society. Lao Tzu's analogy in this passage, however, encompasses the damage that leaders will suffer when they exercise authority that does not reside either in themselves or in the organization. Any laws, restrictions, or punishments that inhibit the natural growth and independent development of the human mind will destroy both the organization and its leaders.

是謂代大匠斲。夫代大匠斲者。希有不傷其手矣

吾得執而殺之孰敢?常有司殺者殺。夫代司殺者殺。

民不畏死。奈何以死懼之?若使民常畏死而爲奇者。

MISFORTUNE

"Misfortune comes by means of the mouth" is an old Chinese proverb. It implies that troubles are often brought on by oneself. The character for misfortune (凶) *shows a human (人) falling headlong (乂) into a pit (凵).*

SELF-DESTRUCTIVE LEADERSHIP

People are hungry.
    Because those above consume too much in taxes,
    People are hungry.

People are difficult to lead.
    Because those above interfere with them,
    People are difficult to lead.

People make light of death.
    Because those above deeply seek survival,
    People make light of death.

Indeed, it is those who do not interfere with life
Who are capable of respecting life.

Lao Tzu wrote the *Tao Te Ching* during an era when the separate states of China were vying with one another for political supremacy. In observing the rulers and the lives of their subjects, he saw a pattern that he describes in this passage. Unevolved leaders tend to develop a deep fear of losing their position, and they identify that fear with the interests of the organization. As a result they take extraordinary defensive measures to "protect" the organization, and they impose regulations that restrict the livelihood of the people. The people, in paying for their leader's fears, do not get enough to eat. They become inured to the killing of other humans, and they develop a growing contempt for their leader. Lao Tzu notes that organizations that interfere with the instincts of the people and do not support their basic needs cannot endure for long.

BAMBOO IN SNOW BY K'UO PI

In Chinese lore, bamboo is emblematic of longevity because of its great strength, its usefulness, and its ability to flourish in winter. It is the most versatile of all plants and is used in China for food, paper, housing, and medicine. The thousand and one uses of bamboo were enumerated in a third-century classic, the
Treatise on Bamboo (Chu P'u).

Bamboo has always been a favorite subject for calligraphers and painters, because its elegant and responsive flexibility allows the artist to experiment with the effects of invisible natural forces, such as wind. The artist K'uo Pi (A.D. 1301 to 1335) was a gifted calligrapher who excelled in using brush and ink to depict bamboo.

The National Palace Museum, Taipei, Taiwan

THE POWER IN FLEXIBILITY

A man living is yielding and receptive.
Dying, he is rigid and inflexible.
All Things, the grass and trees:
    Living, they are yielding and fragile;
    Dying, they are dry and withered.

Thus those who are firm and inflexible
    Are in harmony with dying.
Those who are yielding and receptive
    Are in harmony with living.

Therefore an inflexible strategy will not triumph;
    An inflexible tree will be attacked.
The position of the highly inflexible will descend;
    The position of the yielding and receptive will ascend.

Through their observations of nature, those who follow the Tao know that what survives on earth is that which easily adapts to the changing circumstances in the environment. It is because the universe is evolving that all things in it are developing and changing. Therefore any inflexibility in systems of belief, in patterns of behavior, or in habits of physical or intellectual nourishment, can cause one to respond to external stimuli in a way that leads to extinction. Similar situations should not necessarily elicit the same responses through time — because in time everything changes. Fixed and unintuitive responses will stop personal growth and will put one in harmony with dying. Cultivating flexibility, on the other hand, will fine-tune the instinctive responses, so that one might, indeed, inherit the earth.

The word *strategy* (*ping*) can also be translated as "soldier," "attack," or "arms." The word is commonly used in the context of applied military science. *Ping* was also translated as "attack" in this passage.

76

是以兵強則不勝。木強則兵。強大處下。柔弱處上
故堅強者。死之徒。柔弱者。生之徒
人之生也柔弱。其死也堅強。萬物草木之。生也柔脆。其死也枯槁

DIRECTING THE POWER

The Tao in Nature
    Is like a bow that is stretched.
The top is pulled down,
    The bottom is raised up.
What is excessive is reduced,
    What is insufficient is supplemented.

The Tao in Nature
    Reduces the excessive
    And supplements the insufficient.
The Tao in Man is not so;
    He reduces the insufficient,
    Because he serves the excessive.

Who then can use excess to serve the world?
Those who possess the Tao.

Therefore Evolved Individuals
    Act without expectation,
    Succeed without taking credit,
    And have no desire to display their excellence.

Those who follow the Tao are aware of nature's tendency to balance extremes in the environment. In the ecological plane, nature is adept at pulling down species that grow too dominant and carefully supporting those that are most fragile. On the atomic level, this balancing can be observed in the way that over-charged particles seek out their opposite to stabilize their existence. So too, on the social plateau, individuals who attempt to dominate others trigger a natural psychological response from their society: a collective urge to neutralize the effect of the excessive members. The complement of this response, in group psychology, is the urge to direct help toward individuals who have insufficient means.

Because Evolved Individuals understand this pattern of energy in the universe, they are able to use it to protect their position while they bring progress to their world. So that energy will flow in their direction, they reduce their position by maintaining an atmosphere of moderation and humility in their relations to others. They then use this energy to alter reality through the focus of their attitudes and convictions.

天之道。其猶張弓與。高者抑之。下者舉之。

有餘者損之　天之道。損有餘

而補之。不足者補之　天之道。損有餘

而補不足。人之道則不然。損不足。以奉有餘

孰能有餘以奉天下？唯有道者

是以聖人。爲而不恃。

功成而不處。其不欲見賢

WATER

A natural source of power and transportation, water (水) is written with a broad central stroke ( ) representing a stream or channel. Alongside it are smaller feathery strokes ( ), suggesting the ripples and whorls water forms as it moves.

ACCEPTING THE BLAME

Nothing in the world,
    Is as yielding and receptive as water;
Yet in attacking the firm and inflexible,
    Nothing triumphs so well.
Because of what it is not,
    This becomes easy.

The receptive triumphs over the inflexible;
    The yielding triumphs over the rigid.
None in the world do not know this.
    None have the ability to practice it.

Therefore Evolved Individuals say:
    One who accepts the disgrace of the organization
    Can be called the leader of the grain shrine.
    One who accepts the misfortunes of the organization
    Can be called the leader of the world.

Right words appear to reverse themselves.

This passage opens with a familiar image in the *Tao Te Ching*, that of the triumph of water over the hard and inflexible. Water yields and receives, and because it has no edge, no shape, no limits (what it is not), it can absorb and erode firmness and structure. In accepting blame, Evolved Leaders willingly yield, taking on the soft, receptive qualities of water that lead to ultimate triumph. They know that accepting the responsibility for all problems within the organization will stabilize their position and extend their influence. It is this paradox, perhaps, that prompted Lao Tzu to note, "Right words appear to reverse themselves."

    Two forms of blame are mentioned in this passage. One is the blame of disgrace: those mistakes made within the organization. Leaders who accept this responsibility are fit to guide the organization. The other blame is for misfortunes that befall the organization from outside. Leaders who accept this responsibility believe that they have the capacity to foresee and avert such problems. These leaders are fit to guide the world.

The term *grain shrine* comes from ancient times when shrines
devoted to the fertility of the crops were constructed on the land by
its feudal lord. Frequently the shrine contained soil from the capital
of the kingdom.

天下莫。柔弱於水。而攻堅強者。莫之能勝。其無以。易之

弱之勝強。柔之勝剛。天下莫不知。莫能行　是以聖人云。

受國之垢。是謂社稷主。受國不祥　是為天下王　正言若反

KING WEN

King Wen (1231-1135 B.C.) was a feudal prince during the final days of the Shang Dynasty. Although known as a wise and benevolent leader, he was denounced as dangerous to the throne by a jealous marquis. Chou Hsin, the last king of the decaying Shang Dynasty, had him seized and thrown into prison. King Wen passed two years in prison studying the eight trigrams and sixty four hexagrams of the I Ching *before being rescued by his son. When Chou Hsin was toppled by those whom he oppressed, King Wen became the founder of the new Chou Dynasty.*

King Wen made a point of choosing learned and able men as his advisors, and it was during the Chou Dynasty that China developed an enlightened social class, one whose responsibility lay in resolving disputes, promoting social harmony, and encouraging intellectual development. The ideas of Confucius and Lao Tzu were widely circulated, and King Wen and his son, the Duke of Chou, wrote commentaries on the hexagrams of the I Ching, *evolving them into a sophisticated method for decision making based on political and humanitarian considerations.*

The National Palace Museum, Taipei, Taiwan

THE POWER IN NOT TAKING ADVANTAGE

Even when a great resentment is reconciled,
Some resentment must linger.
How can this be made good?

That is why Evolved Individuals
Hold the left side of the contract
And do not censure others.
Those with Power are in charge of the contract;
Those without Power are in charge of resolving it.

The Tao in Nature has no favorites.
It always works through the good person.

Whenever there is an obligation between two individuals, it is the responsibility of the individual in the more powerful position to avert the possibility of lingering resentment: resentment that could cloud future events. When Evolved Individuals hold the "left side of the contract," they realize that they have an opportunity to attract Power through compassionate and generous behavior. They know that if they exercise their advantageous position and demand fulfillment, they will create a resentment that will someday return to bring difficulties to their endeavors. Instead, through magnanimity, they use their advantage to create appreciation and harmony. Thus they pave the way to a future more aligned to their needs. Should the other party not fulfill the obligation, Evolved Individuals gain a profound understanding of when and with whom to enter agreements. Such an understanding will protect them throughout life.

The word *contract* (*ch'i*) comes from an ancient term used to describe bamboo tallies that were inscribed and split in half when a loan was made. The right side was held by the debtor, the left side by the creditor.

FULFILLING INDEPENDENCE

In a small organization with few people;

Let there be ten or a hundred times
    More tools than they can use.
Let the people value their lives
    And yet not move far away.
Even though there are boats and carriages,
    There is no occasion to use them.
Even though there are armor and weapons,
    There is no occasion to display them.

Let the people again knot cords and use them.
    Their food will be pleasing.
    Their clothes will be fine.
    Their homes will be secure.
    Their customs will be joyful.

Nearby organizations may watch each other;
    Their crowing and barking may be heard.
Yet the people may grow old and die
    Without coming or going between them.

In this passage, Lao Tzu describes his view of ideal independent social organizations — whether families, businesses, states, or nations. The ideal organization creates an atmosphere that complements and enhances the development of every member by providing, within the organization, the tools of personal growth: health, education, and recreation. Because the people value the quality of their lives, they must have what they need to fulfill their potential and find themselves. When people are encouraged to observe and monitor their own progress — Lao Tzu calls this "knotting cords" — they develop a strong sense of personal power and independence. They find joy and completion in the basics of life: food, clothing, shelter, and culture. When they are independent and satisfied, they will not stray from their work, from their relationships, or from their loyalties.

The idea of knotting cords comes from a ancient Chinese system of mathematics and memory storage. The knotted ropes might be thought of as a crude circuit board with the knots acting as switches. The abacus was developed from this system.

小國寡民

使有什伯之。器而不用。

使民重死。而不遠徙。雖有舟輿。無所乘之。

雖有甲兵。無所陳之。使人復結繩而用之。

甘其食。美其服。安其居。樂其俗

鄰國相望。雞犬之聲相聞。

民至老死。不相往來

STONE RUBBING OF THE PHILOSOPHER LAO TZU

THE EVOLVED WAY

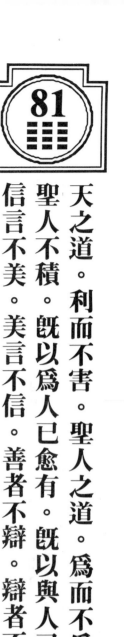

Sincere words are not embellished;
    Embellished words are not sincere.
Those who are good are not defensive;
    Those who are defensive are not good.
Those who know are not erudite;
    Those who are erudite do not know.

Evolved Individuals do not accumulate.
    The more they do for others, the more they gain;
    The more they give to others, the more they possess.

The Tao of Nature
    Is to serve without spoiling.
The Tao of Evolved Individuals
    Is to act without contending.

Reality, integrity, and insight — characteristics cultivated by those on the Way — must not be allowed to become distorted. If the truth is not enhanced and embellished, it has little chance of becoming an illusion; if actions are not quickly justified by words, then good works can shine through; if knowledge goes beyond worldly matters and runs deep into the Self, then wisdom will grow.

Evolved Individuals know that hoarding goods (matter), services (energy), or information is contrary to the laws of nature, and such actions will create a dangerous personal imbalance. In order to continually align themselves with the Tao and stabilize their position within the flow of people and events, they dispense what they have so that more might flow through their hands. They avoid acting in a way that suggests aggressiveness or contention — thus they do not invite counter-reactions that might deflect them from the Way.

天之道。利而不害。聖人之道。爲而不爭
聖人不積。既以爲人已愈有。既以與人已愈多
信言不美。美言不信。善者不辯。辯者不善。知者不博。博者不知